SpringerBriefs in Law

For further volumes:
http://www.springer.com/series/10164

Laura Palazzani

Gender in Philosophy and Law

Springer

Laura Palazzani
Department of Law
Lumsa University
Rome
Italy

Translated by Prof. Victoria Bailes and Marina Fella

ISSN 2192-855X ISSN 2192-8568 (electronic)
ISBN 978-94-007-4990-0 ISBN 978-94-007-4991-7 (eBook)
DOI 10.1007/978-94-007-4991-7
Springer Dordrecht Heidelberg New York London

Library of Congress Control Number: 2012942023
This is a translation from Italian G. Giappichelli Editore s.r.l.
Sex/gender: gli equivoci dell'uguaglianza, Torino, Giappichelli, 2011

© The Author(s) 2012
This work is subject to copyright. All rights are reserved by the Publisher, whether the whole or part of the material is concerned, specifically the rights of translation, reprinting, reuse of illustrations, recitation, broadcasting, reproduction on microfilms or in any other physical way, and transmission or information storage and retrieval, electronic adaptation, computer software, or by similar or dissimilar methodology now known or hereafter developed. Exempted from this legal reservation are brief excerpts in connection with reviews or scholarly analysis or material supplied specifically for the purpose of being entered and executed on a computer system, for exclusive use by the purchaser of the work. Duplication of this publication or parts thereof is permitted only under the provisions of the Copyright Law of the Publisher's location, in its current version, and permission for use must always be obtained from Springer. Permissions for use may be obtained through RightsLink at the Copyright Clearance Center. Violations are liable to prosecution under the respective Copyright Law.
The use of general descriptive names, registered names, trademarks, service marks, etc. in this publication does not imply, even in the absence of a specific statement, that such names are exempt from the relevant protective laws and regulations and therefore free for general use.
While the advice and information in this book are believed to be true and accurate at the date of publication, neither the authors nor the editors nor the publisher can accept any legal responsibility for any errors or omissions that may be made. The publisher makes no warranty, express or implied, with respect to the material contained herein.

Springer is part of Springer Science+Business Media (www.springer.com)

Introduction

'Gender' denotes both the conceptual category referring to things or persons that have essential properties in common and that differ in inessential properties (analogously to kind, species, class, type, from the Latin *genus*), and the grammatical category distinguishing between masculine and feminine (in some languages from neuter too). In the first meaning 'gender' refers to human kind; in the second to male/female distinction. At a linguistic and semantic level the structural ambiguity of the term is evident, as it can be used both to indicate the individuals belonging to the human species (insofar as possessing common features, that is having reason, differently from other animal and vegetable species), including males and females, and to indicate the male/female distinction.

Just to complicate the matter, there is the added fact that in the sphere of feminist and feminine thought 'gender' is often used to indicate women, privileging the peculiarity of the female condition in the use of the term, considered historically, socially and culturally disadvantaged with respect to the male one and therefore in need of special consideration. The use of the word in reference to some disciplines has become widespread (for example, gender politics, gender rights, gender economics, gender sociology, gender medicine, gender pharmacology, etc.) to denote the need for a specific consideration of women in the different sectors of knowledge and practice.

Therefore, 'gender' means human gender, male/female gender, female gender. The word 'gender' presents several meanings. One could be tempted to resolve the problem summarily by referring to the 'generic character' of the term as vague, imprecise, indefinite and indeterminate and indeterminable. And yet, as can clearly be seen, the proof of the vagueness of the English term gender may be identified in the difficulty or even impossibility to translate it into Italian, French, Spanish and German. *Gender*—only in the English language—can be clearly distinguished from *genre* or *kind* which means species and type. So what does it mean exactly?

In Anglo-Saxon literature, the sphere of development of the category, the crux in order to understand gender is to place it in relation to sex: sex denotes the biological condition of man and woman, of the male or female being (how one is born); gender denotes the interior psychological perception of one's own identity (how one feels), but also the exterior social, historical and cultural condition (how one appears to others), in the behaviour, habits and roles that are given and assumed by masculinity and femininity. Sex denotes how we are, the natural condition; gender denotes how we become, the acquired condition.

But what is the relationship between sex and gender? There are various answers to this.

One naïve answer is given by those who consider that the meaning of the two terms coincides indifferently, thinking that gender is only a different and preferable expression with respect to sex, since it is more polite and refined. The word sex, evoking the sexual relationship, can sound vulgar. This is a naïve answer as it does not take into account, unconsciously through ignorance, but perhaps consciously and intentionally, a structured theoretical debate between biological determinism (that reduces gender to sex), social constructionism (that separates gender from sex) and deconstructionism (that thematises the priority of gender over sex). In other words, the debate among those who consider that there is and must be a correspondence between sex and gender, between how we are and how we become, and those who maintain that there may be no correspondence between sex and gender, that we can become different from how we are born. In short, the debate between those on the side of nature, claiming the priority of sex over gender and those on the side of culture, maintaining the priority of gender over sex.

The question becomes even more complex when one considers that, following the widening of scientific knowledge, the determination of the sex refers not only to what appears at the moment of birth, but also to the analysis of the genetic, gonadic, hormonal, morphological and anatomic dimension with reference to primary and secondary sexual characteristics, and that these dimensions may not correspond. The cases of children born with genital ambiguities or sexual indeterminacy (but also those of adults who discover the incongruity between their acquired identity and genetic sexual belonging) are empirical proof of this. In this context, gender is separated from sex to denote an identity that is moulded by education, oriented in a feminine or masculine direction, following a medical transformation of the body in the search for a difficult sex/gender correspondence. It is no coincidence that the distinction between sex and gender was born in the sphere of psycho-sexology, to look for a theoretical and practical answer in such difficult cases: the variability of the gender made it possible to explain identification even in cases of sex reassignment. Such distinction returns in psychoanalysis to explain sexual identification as the gradual process of the acquisition of gender identity in correspondence or contrast with the sex, also in reference to transsexualism, or in cases of the non-correspondence between the sex embodied and the gender experienced psychologically.

The debate by psycho-sexology and psychoanalysis was taken up by a number of feminist orientations with different modalities and arguments at a sociological, cultural-anthropological and philosophical level, to try and find the cause of the disadvantaged condition of women in history, society and culture. According to some feminist theories, the way in which gender was constructed, or the cultural and social expectations towards women and the assigning of roles to women linked to their biological condition, led to a hierarchisation of the sexes and to the subordination of women with respect to men. A different new construction of gender at a social and cultural level which sets aside sex is seen as a possibility to conquer a position, if not of advantage, at least of equality and symmetry with respect to men. In this sense the use of reproduction technologies is considered, in this perspective, as a way for women to have children without a partner, without pregnancy and without childbirth. It is called 'gender revolution', like a sort of second sexual revolution: while the first was aimed at the sexual liberation from inhibitions and repressions of moral norms for the affirmation of free love transforming 'politics into sex', the second revolution transforms 'sex into politics', modifying sexual politics in the direction of a transformation of the sexual relationship understood as a relationship of power, dominion/subordination. Gender studies which substitute the traditional 'women's studies' are on the rise: the former are sometimes used in the meaning of the latter, sometimes denoting a different context of research, delineating the paths of gender feminism.

The real challenge and strong provocation of the *gender* category however is to be found in the passage from modern to postmodern thought. A far from clear passage: in certain aspects anticipated or prophesised by modern theorisations, but expressed in its radicalism and made explicit in its extreme consequences in the postmodern. It is in this context that gender, already previously set free from sex, separates more and more and multiplies itself in the 'differences', strictly and intentionally declined in the plural. Gender becomes a category next to that of race, class and ethnic group.

It is in this context that gender is linked to sexuality, understood not only as erotic attraction, but also as ties of affection and sentiments. Gender denotes not only individual psychological, social and cultural identity acquired regardless of sex, but also sexual orientation (the expressions are often considered synonymic), or the choice and preference with respect to the relationship with the other person of the same sex, opposite sex, but also of both sexes. Here arises the debate on heterosexuality, homosexuality and bisexuality, but also on all the other sexual preferences in the 'sexuality studies'.

In postmodern thought post-gender theorisations are put forward. 'Post-gender' means 'beyond' gender, de-constructing both sex and gender, claiming a distancing from nature which is considered irrelevant but also from culture, thought to be the cause of 'normalisation' as well as of 'naturalisation', that is of the restrictive suffocating imposition of assumed cooped up roles in a just as much assumed nature. To deconstruct means un-doing sex and gender, extolling the even transitory instinctive pulsionality of multiple and plural identities, both male and female or neither male nor female identities (trans-gender), considering any homo/hetero/bisexuality equivalent. This is the perspective that rises against every paradigm that may claim the conformation and standardisation to a hetero-sexual social model, producing stigmatisation and violence. It is the exaltation of in-difference, of neutrality and neutralisation which ends up denying identity itself. 'Post-gender' includes also cyborgs, bio-virtual entities that dis-identify themselves and perhaps do not even really exist.

It is in postmodern thought that the gender category brings with it the problematisation of sexual binarism, which considers that the sexes are two and opposite. And also the contestation of heterosexism, that declares the privilege of unions between the two opposite sexes. On the contrary, the post-gender theories exalt sexual polymorphism, declaring the existence of the third, fourth, fifth sex and pansexualism, which admits any tie between sexes, similar and opposite, where age, number or preference do not count.

These are not sophisticated far-fetched theories. It is sufficient to read some recent newspaper reports: for the first time in Australia a man/woman asked for the registration of a neuter sex; in Canada two parents have not revealed the sex of their son/daughter with the intention of raising him/her 'without sex' so that he/she can decide freely.

These theories or facts are undoubtedly extremely provocative. It is not easy to outline the developments of the gender debate, owing to its inter-disciplinarity, the frequent non-systematic nature, and the style which intentionally forgets, hides and does not express the reasoning clearly. It is indispensable to go back to the origins of the use of the word and to go carefully over the different theorisations, in order to understand what is behind the use of the gender category in today's debate.

Why make this conceptual effort?

One could be tempted to avoid the issue. We do not generally ask ourselves whether we are men or women. We are and that is it. We are born and grow with an awareness that we take for granted, making no issue out of it. And yet, today it is not sufficient to appeal to experience, to reality and say: if I am born a woman, I am a woman and I become a woman; if I am born a man, I am a man and I become a man. Only men and women exist: the rest are mere mental lucubrations, sophisticated and abstruse and do not matter a great deal. The course considered 'normal' or 'natural' is not and cannot be taken for granted.

The reality is more complex than it might seem. The cases of sexual ambiguity at birth show that even the determination of the biological sex is not univocal; the cases of the psychological non-recognition of one's identity in the body (transsexualism); the provocative cases, which are no longer so rare, of the trans-gender claim of neutral identity are increasing. Not in the weak sense of having the behaviour and identification of social roles: women who behave in a masculine way or men who behave in a feminine way. But in the strong sense, in the transformation of the body in the acceptance or exaltation of the ambiguity presenting both male and female features, or perhaps neither male nor female ones.

Neutrality and in-difference also affects the relationship between individuals, delineating a comparability and comparison between hetero/homo/bisexuals. Not only every choice with respect to their own sexual identity, but also the sexual preference with respect to the other, belonging to the opposite sex or to the same sex is considered equivalent. The relationships of men with men, women with women (also more than two), of transsexual and transgender persons with each other are considered equivalent. Everything becomes indistinct and undistinguishable. Every attempt to make a distinction is seen and rejected as being suffocating, oppressive and repressive. The gender category is substituted with queer to denote how the diversity must not be considered 'strangeness', but must be considered 'normality', cancelling any distinction between normal and abnormal by the very denial of every diversity. Instead, normalising abnormality.

The complexity of the reality forces us to think. Are males and females really different? To what extent and how are they different? Does it matter how we are born or what we become? Can we be women and become men or vice versa be men and become women? Can we be neutral, neither men nor women or men and women? Is the fact that a certain identity is given to males and females and a role according to their anatomy a natural fact or a convention? Or is it a socio-cultural construction from which to free oneself? Is sexual preference equivalent at a social level? Is the hetero/homo/bisexual choice indifferent? What is the meaning of diversity at individual level and what are the implications in interpersonal relations? What is the source of individual and relational diversity, biology, culture or individual will?

These are all questions which, if taken seriously, are devastating at a theoretical and existential level. This is the reason why it is important to make a conceptual effort and reflect on the gender category and above all to ask oneself these questions and then look for an answer.

The question cannot be avoided: what is gender? It can now be understood why the answer to this question cannot be naïve. It is an answer that is intellectually demanding, insofar as it forces one to take a stance with respect to reality, to compare the theories in this field and make a choice, not on the basis of emotions, but of reasons, reasoning and justifications. It is an attitude that has significant implications on the way of understanding the body, subjectivity, identity; on the way of understanding relationality, family and society.

The gender theorisations are known, thematised and debated only by experts in the academic world and undoubtedly ignored by public opinion and perhaps also by some experts in the sector. Nonetheless, these theories have already begun to produce effects at a juridical, social and political level, perhaps playing on that very ambiguity and the non immediate understanding of the language. A real silent paradigmatic subversion is even suggested, insofar as it inadvertently creeps into the law and society. It is manifested not in collective physical violence promoted by a structured organised movement, but with the perhaps more sophisticated elaboration of a vision of the world that works towards the spreading of ideas, infiltrating educational, cultural and political institutions, with the aim of transforming society. The so-called 'gender agenda' or 'gender mainstreaming' is a social, juridical and political programme.

The words 'gender ideology' or 'genderology' are also used, to denote the studies that have debated this issue in reference to gender identity but also to the ideology underpinning it. By ideology is meant a structured and coherent system of ideas formulated and theorised at a philosophical level, which is proposed as a total interpretation of the social and historical reality for the purpose of realising a transformation in the utopia of the perfect society, presupposing a passage from theory to practice, in the direction of a transformation of society according to the theory proposed as social model. The gender ideology proposes the theorisation of the irrelevance of nature for sexual identity and the irrelevance of sexual difference for the setting up of the family, exalting freedom as a product of individual desire: in short, a 'sexless society', but perhaps also 'a society without sexes' (at least the two traditional ones), without sexual identity and without sexual difference.

This is the reason for making the conceptual effort of understanding the sex/gender/sexuality debate. Today it is important to reconstruct the debate, understand its lines of thought and discuss them critically, to understand if it still makes sense to root sexual identity in nature, whether sexual difference in the relationship still has a sense.

This volume sets out to analyse the different theories that have dealt with the gender category, highlighting the theoretical and philosophical aspects (the conceptual premises, the lines of reasoning and the vision of the world from which they depart), with particular attention to the sex/gender dichotomy, outlining the philosophically important concepts. The issue is extremely complex and structured, the literature vast and difficult to keep up with owing to its continuous evolution. Attention has been paid to the most important theories at philosophical level, without any claim to being an exhaustive study. The main reference is to the Anglo-Saxon literature in which the debate is particularly developed, with references to the international one too. The developments are traced in the sphere of a line of continuity between modern and postmodern, from weak interpretations to strong ones, considering also intermediate stances.

The further delimitation of the field is disciplinary: the sex/gender debate is structurally interdisciplinary, referring to the scientific areas of genetics, biology, endocrinology, anatomy, physiology, neurology and to the field of human sciences of history, sociology, cultural anthropology, psychology, psycho-sexology, psychoanalysis, but also of linguistics, pedagogy, literature, communications, to the inclusion of the practical areas of economics, politics and law. Greater space has been dedicated in this analysis to philosophical authors and studies, bearing in mind the contributions to the theorisations from the other disciplines, particularly from psychoanalysis, social psychology, sociology, cultural anthropology, all strictly connected with philosophy. The analysis focuses on a number of conceptual constants, even though declined with different grades and meanings, the most significant, representative and influential theories in the philosophical debate, which have had repercussions on the field of the ethical and juridical debate. Particular reference will be made to the recurrent applicative issues: intersexuality, transsexualism, transgender, homosexuality, bisexuality.

The aim is to offer a systematic framework, a sort of conceptual orientation map in the complexity of the debate, in an effort to identify the various aspects and development processes of the theories, so as to highlight the conceptual elements of the theorisations to grasp the problem areas within them. It is therefore an overall synthetic and also explicative analysis, but not only explicative: the aim is to outline the arguments supporting the different theories and the counter-arguments too, for the purpose of proposing categories to weigh up the elements and to take one's own critical stance, with a methodological style that is neither descriptive nor prescriptive, but critical. Not limiting oneself to pointing out 'what one thinks', nor claiming or imposing 'what one must think', but seeking to identify 'what it is possible to think' for the purpose of taking a personal standpoint on the subject, that is dialectically and critically justified.

In the case of gender we find ourselves before a direct passage 'from' philosophy 'to' law, without any (or anyway little) social and cultural mediation: in the juridical context the introduction of the term without any explanation is evident. In order to understand the explanation it is necessary to analyse the philosophical debate, which is generally not always clear. No one has ever pointed out or wanted to explain the reason for this linguistic modification and what it involves. This volume has set out to investigate the reasons for such choice, in order to verify its theoretical consistency, and therefore also its coherence in practical translatability. Moving from the de-construction of gender to a possible philosophical and philosophical-juridical re-construction, of the relevance of nature in sexual identity and of sexual difference in the family relationship. The goal is to demonstrate the dangers of an in-different law, the contradictions and ambiguities that arise behind the appeals to equality and non-discrimination, in order to comprehend and justify the sense of the fundamental human rights of the person before the gender claims.

Contents

1 **From 'Sex' to 'Gender': Origins and Paths of Theorisation** 1
  1.1 Paths of Psychosexology and Psychoanalysis 2
      1.1.1 Money: The Plasticity of Gender 2
      1.1.2 Stoller: Core Gender Identity 8
      1.1.3 Freud's Contribution to the Theory
            of Gender Identity........................... 11
  1.2 Sociological Paths 13
      1.2.1 Doing Gender................................ 13
      1.2.2 Gender as a Social Construction................. 16
      1.2.3 Gender as a Cultural Construction................ 18
  1.3 Philosophical Paths of Feminism....................... 22
      1.3.1 From Equality/Difference to the Question
            of Sex/Gender 22
      1.3.2 Women are Like Men: Oppression
            as a Matter of Gender 24
      1.3.3 Rethinking: the Second Sex Questions
            Nature and Culture 27
      1.3.4 The Sexual Revolution: Women Beyond Their
            Biological Destiny............................ 29
      1.3.5 Lesbian Separatism 32

2 **From Gender to Queer** 35
  2.1 Gender Between Modern and Postmodern 35
      2.1.1 A Paradigm Shift in Gender..................... 35
      2.1.2 The Multiplication of Differences:
            Intersections of Gender 38
      2.1.3 Un-Doing Gender: The Queer Category............ 40
  2.2 Post-gender and Post-queer........................... 48
      2.2.1 J. Butler: Undoing Gender...................... 48
      2.2.2 T. De Lauretis: Sui Generis 54
      2.2.3 D. Haraway: Cyborgs 56

3 Gender: From Theory to Law ... 59
3.1 Lines of International Declarations and Provisions ... 59
3.1.1 From the Conference of Cairo and Beijing ... 60
3.1.2 The Yogyakarta Principles ... 62
3.1.3 Other Documents ... 63
3.2 Lines of European Regulations ... 65
3.2.1 Provisions ... 65
3.2.2 Sentences and Documents ... 67
3.3 A Look at European Legislations ... 69

4 Identity and Equality in Sexual Difference ... 73
4.1 Male or Female: The Reasons for Sexual Binarism ... 73
4.1.1 A Person is Born Male or Female: The Non-malleability of Gender ... 73
4.1.2 Sexual Identity as Constitutive of the Self ... 76
4.1.3 The Sexes are Two: Neither Many Nor One Nor None ... 78
4.1.4 One Becomes a Woman or Man, if She/He Already is ... 80
4.1.5 The Variability of the Gender Identity ... 82
4.1.6 Transsexualism as the Search for Sex/Gender Harmony ... 84
4.1.7 The Intersex Condition and Transgender as a Problem ... 85
4.2 The Dialectic of the Sexes: The Reasons for Complementarity ... 87
4.2.1 Sexual Difference in the Relationship ... 87
4.2.2 Heterosexuality as Straight Orientation: The Generation ... 88
4.2.3 The 'Rainbow Family' as a Problem ... 90
4.3 Gender Between Equality and Non Discrimination ... 93
4.3.1 The Ambiguities of Equality: Treating Equals Equally and the Unequal Unequally ... 93
4.3.2 Women and Men: Equal and Different Before the Law ... 94
4.3.3 The LGBTI Claims: Equality as Equivalence ... 97
4.3.4 The Claim of the Aggravating Circumstance for Offences of Homophobia and Transphobia as a Problem ... 100
4.3.5 The Law Cannot and Must Not be Indifferent ... 102

Glossary ... 105

Selected Bibliography on 'Sex/gender' Debate ... 111

Chapter 1
From 'Sex' to 'Gender': Origins and Paths of Theorisation

Abstract The origin of the word 'gender', as opposed to the word 'sex', is controversial. For some it dates back to psychosexology (J. Money, R.J. Stoller) and psychoanalysis (S. Freud); for others to social psychology and sociology (theories of 'doing gender', gender socialisation and social constructionism); still others date it to feminism. The reconstruction of the origin and use of the term 'gender' across different disciplines reveals how, even in the heterogeneity of thematisations, a theoretical common thread emerges: the progressive removal of 'gender' from 'sex' against the theory of biological determinism which presupposes the identification of sex and gender. This separation is introduced with arguments, for different reasons and purposes. Gender is increasingly being characterised as the category of malleability and variability as opposed to the fixity and immobility of sex. Such progressive separation marks the irrelevance of sex and nature, which is placed at the margins. The estrangement from nature assumes different meanings: that of being the solution to empirical problematicity, but also of liberation from the female condition.

Keywords Sex/gender · Biological determinism · Social constructivism · Doing gender · Gender socialisation · Feminism · Gender role · Gender identity

The origin of the word 'gender', as opposed to the word 'sex', is controversial. For some it dates back to psychosexology and psychoanalysis; for others to social psychology and sociology; still others date it to feminism. Thematisation of the category follows paths in the spheres of epistemologically distinct disciplines, which present some theoretically significant common elements.

1.1 Paths of Psychosexology and Psychoanalysis

1.1.1 Money: The Plasticity of Gender

John Money is often identified as having introduced the term 'gender'.[1] Money considered himself as the first to have used this expression, or at least to have defined it in a scientific journal.[2] The author introduces the expression conscious of its recent and popular spread and that there is no unanimity in meaning. He himself speaks of "nosologic chaos" in terminology and international conceptualisation, expressing the need to "bring order" seeking a common language in the spheres of genetics, endocrinology, neuroendocrinology, sexology, psychology, psicosexology, psychoanalysis, psychiatry, and behaviorism.

Reconstructing the history of the use of the term 'gender', the author distinguishes between 'gender' and 'sex', believing that gender also includes sex, but is not restricted to it. Money recognises that the need for a precise definition of gender in relation to sex emerges from the empirical study of hermaphroditism: studies on this phenomenon reveal the "terrible strain" imposed (or that we impose in the use of language) by the etymological root of the word 'sex'.[3] The term 'sex' has multiple uses, all of which are solely attributed to the physical meaning of the genetic, gonadal, hormonal, genital, morphological condition or to the meaning associated with civil or legal status; in this sense it is used for sexual classification. The author introduces the gender category as a broad concept that includes sex in a physical sense, but he goes beyond this, making a distinction between 'gender role' and 'gender identity'. These are different aspects of the same thing, one being the "counterpart" of the other.[4]

Gender role is defined as "everything that a person says and does, to indicate to others or to the self the degree that one is either male, or female, or ambivalent";[5] or also "to disclose himself or herself as having the status of boy or man, girl or

---

[1] J. MONEY, *Gendermaps: Social Constructionism, Feminism, and Sexosophical History*, Continuum, New York 2002; J. MONEY, A.A. EHRHARDT, *Man & Woman, Boy and Girl. The Differentiation and Dimorphism of Gender Identity from Conception to Maturity*, John Hopkins University Press, Baltimore 1972; J. MONEY, P. TUCKER, *Sexual Signatures. On Being a Man or a Woman*, Little, Brown and Company, London-Toronto 1975, p. 86.

[2] J. MONEY, *Hermaphroditism, Gender and Precocity in Hyperadreno-corticism: Psychologic Findings*, "Bullettin of John Hopkins Hospital", 1955, 96 (6), pp. 253-264.

[3] The word 'sex', Money notes, has only five derivative forms in the English language: sexes, sexed, sexual, sexually, sexuality. No other terms can be derived such as sexuous, sexitive, sexible, sexitise etc. (similar to the many derivatives, up to thirty, of the term, sense, such as sensuous, sensitive, sensible, sensitise, but also sensate, sensation, sensor, sentient etc.). Cf. J. MONEY, *Gender: History, Theory and Usage of the Term in Sexology and its Relationship with Nature/Nurture*, "Journal of Sexual and Marital Therapy", 1985, 11, pp. 71–79.

[4] Money opened the Gender Identity Clinic in Baltimore.

[5] J. MONEY, A.A. EHRHARDT, *Man and Woman, Boy and Girl*, cit.

woman, respectively".[6] "All those things" refers to words or actions and in particular to the general peculiarities of behaviour and conversation, direct and indirect questions and answers, as well as sexual practices.[7] These thoughts, words and actions indicate the social assumption of roles, that is, 'how we should behave' in terms of what is considered appropriate or what is expected in a certain socio-cultural context. Gender identity is the "sense of self, the unity and persistence of individuality male or female, or ambivalent, in greater or lesser degree, particularly as the experience of gendered perceptions of oneself and one's behaviour".[8] *Gender* is therefore a psychosocial category that expresses characteristics, attitudes and feelings that are appropriate to masculine and feminine.[9]

The conceptualisation of gender goes 'beyond' sex in a meta-biological perspective, as an external and public expression (what is observed in the social, historical and cultural environment) and a perception attemptable internally and privately (what one feels inside). "Gender identity is the personal experience of gender role, and the role linked to gender is the external expression of gender identity".[10] The two dimensions may or may not coincide. The non-coincidence goes back to the problem of separating the body/mind, which is part of the wider and more general distinction of nature/culture, innate/acquired, instinctive/learned.

From analysis of these definitions it emerges that Money's theoretical perpective lies in the context of the 'nature/nurture' debate, between biological determinism/innatism and biological indeterminism or environmental determinism, with reference to the definition of the degree of influence of biological and environment factors on the formation of human identity and behaviour. Biological determinism is the thesis that physical sex (which includes the genetic, hormonal, gonadal, anatomical, and biological dimension) determines gender[11] from birth in a static, fixed, irrevocable and unchangeable manner. It is a theory not only in line with evolutionism and sociobiology, but even with innatism, that considers gender pre-determined in sex and with the naturalism/essentialism (nature theory). This philosophical theory asserts that nature constitutes, as innate substrate, the essence of gender identity postulated as coinciding with sex. Biological indeterminism is

---

[6] J. Money, *Gender Role, Gender Identity, Core Gender Identity: Usage and Definition of Terms*, "Journal of the American Academy of Psychoanalysis", 1973, 1 (4), p. 397.

[7] Money refers to his having felt the need for the concept and its definition in a seminar in 1949 where George Gardner Harvard presented the case of a hermaphrodite. This was a case, now known as the syndrome of non-sensitivity to androgens in a chromosomally male individual (46, XY) with external female morphology, but genetically male. Money wrote a doctoral thesis on *Hermaphroditism: an Inquiry into the Nature of a Human Paradox* in 1952.

[8] J. Money, A.A. Ehrhardt, *Man & Woman, Boy and Girl*, cit., p. 18. The author distinguishes gender identity from "profound gender identity" which refers, in the context of psychoanalysis, to self-perception as male or female in the second year of life, before the Oedipus complex (*ibid.*, p. 293).

[9] Money indicates it as G-I/R (*Gender, Identity and Role*).

[10] J. Money, *Sex Research: New Developments*, Holt, Rinehart and Winston, New York 1965.

[11] J. Money, P. Tucker, *Sexual Signatures. On Being a Man or a Woman*, cit., p. 3. The author speaks of sex as "unalterable fact" and "eternal truth".

the thesis which maintains that sex is undifferentiated at birth. Environmental determinism (of which the nurture theory is a thematization)[12] states that it is the environment that determines gender, that is, it allows for sexual differentiation as male and female through apprehending inner psychological identity and through exterior social acquisition. Gender, in this perspective, derives from the normal association of roles, imprinted by the family, induced by society and conveyed by the appertaining culture.

According to Money gender role/identity is neither entirely constituted by intrinsic nature (as it is not exclusively a 'being'), nor entirely by the external environment (as it is not exclusively a 'becoming'). He proposes the interactionist theory, according to which gender is structured both with reference to the physical sex of the body and in relation to the inner psyche influenced by the external environment.

The author describes the acquisition of gender as role and identity in the context of the observation of the differentiation of sex from fertilisation to birth. This occurs in relation to a sequence of stages of development, similar to a "relay race", according to a program of sexual dimorphism controlled by sex chromosomes[13] that inform the undifferentiated gonads; gonadal differentiation, in turn, produces the hormonal differentiation, whose presence or absence induces the formation of external genitalia, which also affect brain organisation and consequently sexual behaviour. Morphology is usually decisive for sexual assignment by the physician, education by parents, perception of the individual, as well as for the registration of birth on the formal-legal level.[14]

Money points out how the phylogenetically codified program of *sex* is interwoven with the biographical and social dimension of gender in the context of the narrow nurture theory that identifies specific 'agents of socialisation', referring primarily to the family and secondarily to society. From start to finish the process of differentiation is the product of a set of components, prenatal and postnatal: each one acts and impresses stable and permanent effects, together or separately. It is not possible to clearly and strictly distinguish the biological and psychological components, that are innate and acquired.

According to Money's interactionist perspective determinations or pre-determined programming do not exist in the body, but rather there are dispositions or predispositions which, through external stimuli, allow the progressive acquisition of specific roles and identities. Manhood and womanhood are not two roads, but only one with many bifurcations: at each bifurcation one can choose the male or female direction of becoming a man or woman, based on what is produced by the interaction.

The interaction is constructed from observation of reality and through the experiences induced by education that form in the brain internal thought patterns

---

[12] This is a popular theory in the sphere of psychology, sociology and anthropology.

[13] The sperm has an X or Y chromosome, while the egg has always an X chromosome, and when an X chromosome sperm fertilises an egg, a genetically female XX individual is produced, when the sperm carrying the Y chromosome fertilises the egg a genetically male XY embryo is produced.

[14] J. MONEY, A.A. EHRHARDT, *Man & Woman, Boy and Girl*, cit., pp. 17–18.

on what it means to be male or female and role models that are validated/invalidated by the approval/disapproval of the external environment. The interaction consists of continuous and constant exchange between the individual and society which progressively exerts an "impetus" through education, socialisation, culturalisation in the context of heredity/environmental interchange. Thought patterns and behaviour patterns, in the opinion of the author, are structured on the basis of identification (the individual identifies with the behaviour of the same sex) and complementarity (the individual compares with a different sex and behaviour). These patterns are assimilated by the brain: one is labelled positively (identification, that is, what we are), and the other negatively (complementarity, that is, what we are not).

The role and identity of gender are formed, according to the author, in parallel with the acquisition of language. Just as language learning depends on the predisposition towards communication and the influence of the external environment, sexual differentiation/identification is in reference to internal factors and external signals. Growth is described in five stages: from prenatal to childhood, from early to late childhood, from puberty to adolescence until adulthood. Money identifies between the ages of eighteen months and three/four years (notwithstanding individual variability)[15] the "critical moment" for gender identification: first the "gate" is open, then it gradually closes. Any subsequent changes affect the psychic balance of the individual. Money, therefore, denies both the determination and indetermination of gender, affirming the plasticity of unarbitrary gender identity, guided by natural predispositions and influenced by external elements. The author recognises that the process of differentiation of sex may undergo prenatal alterations due to internal factors (chromosomal, gonadal, hormonal, morphological) or external alterations (administration of drugs, intrauterine trauma or viral infections) and that the process of identification of gender may include postnatal changes due to the events of personal history and social biography.

In this context, Money analyses the problem of hermaphroditism,[16] which he also calls "intersex".[17] Hermaphrodite is defined by the author as "a person born

---

[15] J. Money, J.G. Hampson, J.L. Hampson, *An Examination of Some Basic Sexual Concepts: the Evidence of Human Hermaphroditism*, "Bulletin of John Hopkins Hospital", 1955, 97, pp. 301–319.

[16] J. Money, J.G. Hampson, J.L. Hampson, *Hermaphroditism: Recommendations Concerning Assignment of Sex, Change of Sex, and Psychologic Management*, "Bulletin of the John Hopkins Hospital", 1955, 97, pp. 284–300.

[17] For Money hermaphroditism is synonymous with intersex: the latter term refers to cases with apparent genetic etiology, but not clearly known (J. Money, A.A. Ehrhardt, *Man & Woman, Boy and Girl*, cit., p. 20). The author also refers to the analysis of hermaphroditism in S. Freud (*Drei Abhandlungen zur Sexualtheorie* (1905), English translation *Three Essays on the Theory of Sexuality*, Basic Books. New York 2000). In the first essay on *The Sexual Aberrations*, with reference to the sexual object, Freud cites anatomical hermaphroditism as normally present in males and females, where there are "traces" of the genital organ of the opposite sex, without functionality, as the original disposition of bisexuality (referring to the possible explanation of homosexuality as "psychic hermaphroditism").

without properly differentiated sexual anatomy"[18] because of abnormalities in chromosome dimorphism, hormonal dimorphism, and genital anatomy. Children who are born with this ambiguity or incongruity (as well as children who despite having a determined sex, due to technical incompetence, are in a state of sexual ambivalence)[19] are, in his opinion, a "false problem". These are cases which he considers a sort of "natural experiment" that prove his theory: they may be solved through surgery and subsequently through hormonal intervention in order to change sexual characteristics according to the assignment/reassignment of sex.[20] In these cases sex may be chosen and "imposed" (on the basis of internal and external elements) by the physician on the basis of the technical feasibility[21] and by parents according to their expectations and desires. The important thing is, according to Money, that the decision should be taken quickly, evaluating the various medical and psychosocial factors (such as infections, reproductive and sexual function): the necessary condition being that, as a result of modification of the body, a congruent education should follow.[22]

Money deals with other cases of non-concordance and contrariety between sex and gender, recognising that there are several psychodynamic requirements that can cause a transposition in the relationship between the two, that is more or less long-lasting or intense, episodic or chronic, partial or total. Among these he mentions transsexualism, as adaptation of sex, that is anatomically and hormonally

---

[18] J. MONEY, A.A. EHRHARDT, *Man & Woman, Boy and Girl*, cit., p. 20.

[19] Money, through his studies, aims to provide empirical evidence for the thesis of the plasticity of gender. It is well known the case of two male twins, one of whom John, because of an accident during surgery (during circumcision) at 18 months of age remained free of genitals. Money decided to feminize the child (calling her Joan) and proposed to the parents to bring up the child as a girl. It was, in addition, their being twins, a scientifically interesting case, to see how much sexual identity is determined biologically and socially. But Joan continually showed signs of discomfort; at the age of 13, on discovering the truth, Joan decided to reinstate being male, subjecting the body to many surgical operations to eliminate the signs of feminisation. The disturbance of psychic equilibrium led him to commit suicide at the age of 38 years. Money publicized the case as empirical proof of his theory. In truth, it must be said, that the child was brought up as a male until 18 months and feminised only at the age of 1 and a half: therefore the discomfort would seem to confirm not so much the thesis of plasticity of gender, as that of the importance of educational pressure early on as regards sexual identification. Cf. J. COLAPINTO, *As Nature Made Him. The Boy Who Was Raised as a Girl*, Harper Collins, New York 2001.

[20] If sex is changed immediately after birth it is called 'reannouncement'; if after a few months, it is 'reallocation/reassignment'. Reallocation requires a change in people's behaviour toward the child; reassignment demands a change in the responses from the child.

[21] In cases of ambiguity, given the complexity of reconstruction of functional male genitalia, they preferred the female assignment of sex to the subject, bringing the child up in this sense, regardless of consideration of physical indices (or even infertility or sexual satisfaction). The indication given by Money was therefore for early assignment, in order to promote "oriented" education, even with demolitive and reconstructive surgery and ensuing hormonal therapy at puberty.

[22] In his view, hermaphroditism is empirical evidence that the stage of post-natal identification/ sexual differentiation should be defined within 18 months and is completed at the age of 4 and a half.

considered 'normal' to gender at an adult age and to transvestism, and he also deals with, albeit incidentally, the themes of homosexuality, bisexuality, ambisexuality.

Money's perspective mainly consists in distinguishing the two poles of sexuality: male or female. But not in an absolute way. According to the author, abstract thought is bipolar, using the reasoning of dual logic (light/dark, hot/cold, good/evil, dead/alive, male/female) with a sharp dividing line, while real experience consists of a spectrum between extremes imagined as absolute but with infinite shades and variations in intensity and degrees, where the dividing line can always be shifted depending on the context. In his view, bipolar thinking is useful, but it should be abandoned. In experience one 'becomes' male or female in stages, only gradually and never definitively: differentiation is a process that is never completed and always susceptible to both physical and psycho-social changes. In his view, growth is a gradual adjustment to society: every culture has conventional 'stereotypes' to meet defining male and female roles. If they are too rigid they risk forcing gender identities, if too lax they do not allow configuration: it is desirable, according to Money, that stereotypes are strong enough to support social cooperation but flexible enough to allow for individual development. He recognises that the basic reproductive functions constitute irreducible sexual differences as a condition for the possibility of the survival of humanity.[23] But at the same time, it includes the provocations of the "pioneers of new lifestyles" that go beyond stereotypes, undermining the sense of identity as well as society itself.[24]

The author speaks of these situations, also known as 'mixed-up sex' or 'unsex' as "virtually impossible";[25] and at other times as "rare"[26] situations. He seems to accept them as a possibility, in principle, equivalent to the male/female choice, hoping for a change in language as well as in social practices in line with 'de-genderisation' or cancellation of the gender difference, by the use of the neutral third person. He believes that the scientist must remain "open", and avoid premature and prejudicial closure to different hypotheses. But Money, while opening to the neutral gender, recognises the importance of stable sexual identification in male or female, believing that the male/female oscillation and sexual uncertainty and indeterminacy are hardly acceptable. He argues that "most human beings can not tolerate such biographical inconsistency".[27]

---

[23] The male reproductive function; the function of gestation, breastfeeding and menstruating in women (J. MONEY, P. TUCKER, *Sexual Signatures. On Being a Man or a Woman*, cit., p. 38).

[24] Money speaks of "sexless zombies" and "ambisexual acrobats" as unprecedented challenges to the sexual revolution (*ibid.*, p. 8).

[25] «It is practically impossible for a person to develop any sense of identity at all without identifying as either a male or a female» (*ibid*, pp. 87–88).

[26] «The third possibility is almost unheard of» (*ibid*, p. 107).

[27] J. MONEY, A.A. EHRHARDT, *Man & Woman, Boy and Girl*, cit., p. 32.

1.1.2 Stoller: Core Gender Identity

Along the same lines as Money, albeit in the context of psychoanalysis,[28] Robert J. Stoller[29] distinguishes sex from gender within the distinction/interaction between nature and culture, body/psyche, biology/environment.

According to the author 'sex' indicates the biological component that determines being male or female,[30] as a substrate of human sexual behaviour divided into male and female. Sex (but also sexual) refers to the physical, anatomical and physiological dimension of sex; gender is a term that has a connotation that is "more psychological or cultural than biological",[31] therefore a non biological dimension,[32] rather, primarily psychological and culturally determined.[33] Sex is about what we are, gender is about what we learn through a process that begins at birth, develops gradually in the family and appears in childhood until full maturity in adulthood.[34] Gender refers, properly, to the exhibition, preservation and development of masculinity and femininity, understood as a unity of feelings, thoughts, and behaviour.

Stoller believes that sex and gender are inextricably interconnected and contiguous: this is what is deduced by common sense, which considers them to be virtually synonymous. But, in his opinion, they are not inevitably and necessarily linked, there is no two-way relationship between sex and gender, as they could also be separate and independent.[35] There is usually a correlation between male sex and masculine gender, as well as between female sex and feminine gender. Gender indicates, in his opinion, the "amount of masculinity or femininity", which is located in a person; there is a mixture of both in humans. Normally the boy/man

---

[28] R. REICHE, *Triebschicksal der Gesellschaft. Über den Strukturwandel der Psyche*, Campus Verlag, Frankfurt a.M. 2004. The author points out the oddity that a term such as gender has passed from psychosexology (an observational and behavioral science) to psychoanalysis, as there is usually a certain hostility between the different disciplines (*ibid.*, p. 132).

[29] R.J. STOLLER, *Sex and Gender. On the Development of Masculinity and Femininity*, The Hogarth Press, London 1968; ID., *A Contribution to the Study of Gender Identity*, "International Journal of Psycho-Analysis", 1964, 45, pp. 220-226; ID., *Presentation of Gender*, Yale University Press, New Haven (Conn.) 1985. In 1958 Stoller constituted a research group "Gender Identity Research Project" to study intersexuality and transexualism.

[30] R.J. STOLLER, *Sex and Gender. On the Development of Masculinity and Femininity*, cit., p. viii.

[31] «Gender is a term that has psychological or cultural rather than biological connotations» (*ibid*, p. 9).

[32] Some believe that Stoller introduced the category of gender not Money (cf. A. EDWARDS, *The Sex/Gender Distinction: has it Outlived its Usefulness?*, "Australian Feminist Studies", 1989, 10, pp. 1–12).

[33] R.J. STOLLER, *Sex and Gender. On the Development of Masculinity and Femininity*, cit., p. xiii.

[34] Stoller recalls that Freud identified sexuality not as a matter of inheritance or of a biochemical nature or dependent on organic factors, but dependent on childhood experiences.

[35] *Ibid*, pp. viii-ix.

has a "preponderance" of masculinity and the girl/woman of femininity.[36] But there are cases of "abnormal interpersonal relationships": there may be a masculine male and a feminine female, but also an effeminate male or masculine female.

The author believes that the difficulty of thematisation of the gender category depends on the concept of identity. By 'identity' he means the "organization of those psychic components that maintain awareness of one's existence (…) and the end of the world". He uses the term 'gender identity' as a "working tool", but is keen to stress that he does not intend to defend its use or claim ownership of an often exalted concept "as one of the splendors" of the scientific world. Gender identity means, in his view, conscious or unconscious sense of belonging to one sex or another, or rather to belong to one sex and not the other.[37] Gender role is the role or position in society as regards gender as identity. Therefore, according to Stoller, gender, gender identity and gender role can be considered synonyms, despite their having subtle semantic differences.

The author does not encompass in the problems of the formation of gender identity the "defensive strategies of an individual to protect himself from the traumas of sexual development and gender".[38] These are themes that concern more specifically those that develop after childhood internal conflicts regarding their identity, which has already been previously formed. In his view, the formation of gender identity coincides with the awareness of one's sexual identity, according to the formula "I am male" or "I am female": it occurs in a person usually in the first years of life from 3 to 5/6 years of age.[39] This perspective takes into account the fact that in the postnatal period psychosexual differentiation occurs before the oedipal phase.[40] Subsequently doubts or the desire even to change one's identity may arise: but those doubts and desires presuppose that identity has already been established according to the formula "I want to be female, because I know I'm male" and vice versa. The 'core gender identity', that is, the awareness of being male or female, remains "unchanged during life".[41]

Stoller outlines his theory with the image of two circles or layers around a nucleus. The inner core represents sex with the various body structures (morphological, endocrine, anatomical, etc.); around the nucleus there is the core gender identity arranged in an isomorphic manner (that is, corresponding to the shape of the body) or non-isomorfically (that is, in contrast with the shape of the body); and around this are the representations of the self and the object (gender

---

[36] *Ibid*, p. 9.

[37] *Ibid*, p. 10.

[38] Such as the Oedipus complex, castration anxiety, penis envy, theme highlighted in this area by Freud.

[39] *Ibid*, p. 72.

[40] Precisely after the tactile and oral phase and before the anal and genital phase, and positioned in the so-called phallic phase.

[41] *Ibid*, p. 72.

role or gender role identity). The elements that contribute to the formation of gender identity are, in the opinion of the author: the 'natural' appearance of the anatomy of external genitalia or sign for the parents for ascription to one sex or the other, and the related feeling that accompanies the body in the early stages of development; the parent/child relationship or the expectations of parents regarding the identity of children, their own gender identity and identification by the child with both sexes in pre-oedipal and oedipal development; but, above all, the "biological force".[42]

Stoller believes that gender identity is primarily learned, but that there are "biological forces" that contribute, increase and interfere with its expression.[43] The author postulates the existence of an innate and instinctive impulse that is unchanged and continuous towards femininity or masculinity. This force, in normal cases, works in harmony with the outside world, but it can also, in some contexts, counter anatomy and the environment, in relation to impressed education and interpersonal relationships. Stoller believes that there is empirical evidence, albeit without scientific proof, to support the theoretical postulate that identifies in gender identity[44] a variable power, usually hidden behind the effects of postnatal psychological influences. As there is no scientific endocrinological and neurophysiological proof, it is conceivable that such a force could be the "algebraic sum of the activities of a number of neuroanatomical centres and hierarchies of neurophysiological functions".[45] Stoller acknowledges that he can not be more precise, but outlines a scenario that tends to establish the prevalence of the biological component in the constitution of gender. At least in some individuals the biological force can become a decisive factor that goes beyond anatomy and external influences, despite there being a "tremendous power"[46] of attitudes and behaviours of parents towards their children in the formation of masculinity and femininity.

The author believes that this biological tendency is related to genetic sex: the tendency to masculinity and femininity in males and females is a silent and effective force from the pre-natal period to birth. Biological and environmental influences usually work in harmony. When this does not occur it is the result of an "unfortunate combination" between a weak biological force towards one's gender and the harmful effects of the environment, as in hermaphroditism and transsexualism.[47]

---

[42] *Ibid*, p. 73.

[43] *Ibid*, p. xiii.

[44] In his work Stoller examines various cases of intersex, transsexualism and transvestism. Repeatedly emphasising that his theory is a postulate, which is more an intuition than a certainty.

[45] *Ibid*, p. 74.

[46] *Ibid*, p. 262.

[47] Stoller explicitly excludes the treatment of the homosexual issue (he speaks of it only to the extent that homosexuality affects gender identity, understood as sexual identification as regards the self). He includes, however, the treatment of transvestites.

1.1.3 Freud's Contribution to the Theory of Gender Identity

Sigmund Freud[48] indirectly entered the sex/gender debate. He did not deal explicitly with the issue, but his theory is a point of reference for the thematisation of the two categories and their mutual relationship. In his opinion, one is born biologically male or female and one becomes a man or a woman socially through a process of identification, understood as a gradual realisation that unwinds throughout several phases. Children learn their gender through comparison with their parent's behaviour, specifically with the same-sex parent or the parent of the opposite sex.

The biological distinction is not clear. Freud notes that the male is made up of seminal cells, the female of egg cells.[49] But, in his opinion, anatomy does not mark a clear difference between male and female.[50] There is a hint of "bisexuality", as if the individual was neither male nor female, but always one or the other, and only a little more one or the other.[51]

He maintains that to attain identity an awareness of sexuality is necessary. There is no "self" without "sexual identity" that coincides with the identity of gender as consciousness of belonging to one sex and not the other. Explaining the acquisition of identity in the early years of life is the problem. Freud, against biological determinism, believed that the psychic constitution of the self is the product of a process of sexually different relationships. The child has a 'libido' as biologically amorphous sexual energy, without form or structure, which can take different directions that are not inherently predetermined. In the preoedipal period a symbiotic and undifferentiated relationship is established, between children and mother. In the oedipal period identity of gender is configured through the comparison with parents, sexually different. Parental sexual difference is a structural element of identification of gender, in the Freudian perspective.

---

[48] This is not the place for a critical reconstruction of Freud's thought. The restricted aim is to identify the elements of his theories relevant to the debate on sex/gender, reiterated in subsequent reflections.

[49] S. FREUD, *Three Essays on the Theory of Sexuality*, cit.

[50] Parts of the male sexual apparatus also appear in the women's bodies, though in an 'atrophied state', and vice versa (S. FREUD, *Femininity*, in ID., *Vorlesungen zur Einführung in der Psychoanalyse* (1915-17), English translation, *New Introductory Lectures on Psycho-Analyisis*, W.W. Norton and Company, New York 1990).

[51] *Ibid.*

Initially, Freud outlines a parallel in the attitude of males and females with respect to parents.[52] The Oedipus complex[53] describes the identification of the male gender. The child's unconscious libidinal desire to join incestuously with the mother, expresses itself in the feeling of jealousy towards the father and the desire for his death. The child feels that the father can become aggressive and is afraid (castration anxiety); and this feeling leads to the internalisation of the rule of the father (the prohibiting of the incestuous union with the mother, the repression of sexual desire), the formation of conscience (superego) and identification with the father (abandonment of the idea of union with the mother and separation from the mother). The absence or weakness of one of the two figures, especially the same-sex parent, leaves the Oedipal conflict unresolved and can lead to difficulties in identification of gender.

Freud originally describes the process of identification of the female child in a parallel way to the male child (desire for incestuous union with the mother and identification with the father). Males and females are separated from the mother, despite still desiring the mother, in line with the father. A process of asymmetrical identification between males and females[54] emerges later in Freudian thinking. The development of identification of gender in the girl is more complex: the Oedipal conflict becomes secondary and emerges after a period of intense attachment to the mother. Freud refers to the Electra complex[55] describing a similar and asymmetrical process in girls: the desire to join with the father and to

---

[52] Freud acknowledges that the female-child's first inclination is for the father and the male-child's first inclination is for the mother (cf. *Traumdeutung,* 1899, English translation, *The Interpretation of Dreams*, Basic Books, New York 2010). In successive theorisation he keeps the symmetry between males and females in the Oedipus complex, maintaining that in the girl it is configured in a similar way with the necessary variations. The affectionate attachment of the father, the need to eliminate the mother as superfluous and to occupy her place, is flirtation that already puts in place the means of future womanhood (cf. *New Introductory Lectures on Psycho-Analyisis*, cit., lecture 21).

[53] Oedipus, in the Sophoclean tragedy, kills his father Laius and marries his mother Gioacasta.

[54] He highlights the difference between males and females saying that for the male child the Oedipus complex ends with the threat of castration; for the little girl the castration complex conducts her towards the Oedipus complex.

[55] Electra, in Greek mythology, daughter of Agamemnon and Clytemnestra, helps her brother in the project of killing the mother. The mother, with her lover Aegisthus killed Agamemnon. Electra, discovering the crime, pushed her brother Orestes, after saving him, to avenge his father by killing his mother and lover.

kill the mother.[56] This is a much debated theory in literature.[57] What it reveals in the Freudian perspective, despite the diversity of interpretation, is the emergence of the identity of gender from biological and psycho-social difference as progressive state of consciousness. The factor plays an important role in the sex/gender debate.

1.2 Sociological Paths

1.2.1 Doing Gender

The gender thematisations in the psychosexological and psychoanalytical field, in a weak or strong manner, share the critique of biological determinism[58] that postulates the original aspect of nature and the subordination of society and of essentialism, which claims anteriority, priority and exclusivity of sex with respect to gender. The deterministic-essentialist perspective considers irrelevant even the terminological distinction of sex/gender.[59] The gender theories argue that gender is not absorbed into sex, as nature does not precede and determine society and culture.[60]

Other theories in the sphere of social psychology and sociology put forward, with different topics and methods, criticism of the naturalistic paradigm, thematising the priority of the social assumption of gender role for the perception of gender identity in relation to sex. According to this view, it is society that has a

---

[56] Until the phallic period the girl child thinks she has the same genitalia as her brother, then she develops penis envy accusing her mother of this state of castration. She turns to the father figure as a symbol of strength: the desire for a penis is transformed into the desire to give him a baby as a substitute for the missing genital organ. The child knows that she will not be able to satisfy the father and transfers the affection to other men hoping to satisfy the desire of becoming a mother.

[57] There is no intention to enter into the complex debate on the question of psychoanalysis. In a line of interpretation of Freud there emerges a distinction between male and female as regards identification. The male child aligns with the father in likeness; girls, because of the similarity with the mother, find it more difficult to leave the state of indifferentiation, they are less willing to separate as they are less afraid of becoming women, despite reaching a weaker sense of self in identification. The process is not absolute or complete; there are situations of tension, confusion and ambiguity. Some feminists criticise Freud, arguing that his perspective leads to a vision of male dominance in psychological and social terms, weakening feminine identity and they criticse the lack of symmetry between male and female in the Oedipus complex.

[58] Theory supported by sociobiology and evolutionary psychology, which believe that gender is mechanically inferred from sex.

[59] This theory is also supported by empirical studies, based on neurological, hormonal, developmental or anthropological-cultural grounds.

[60] It is a theory related to the past, specifically to philosophical metaphysical theories. Cf. D.L. ANSELMI, A.L. LAW, *Questions of Gender. Perspectives and Paradoxes*, McGraw-Hill, New York 1998.

decisive influence on the perception of subjective identity.[61] It is the theory of 'gender socialisation' that brings together the perspectives that explain the acquisition of gender as identity through a dynamic process of socialisation or social learning that leads to a certain way of feeling inwardly and acting outwardly. These theories, albeit in the context of different but closely related disciplines, are confined to the narrow nurture theory, which affirms that society configures and shapes the process of development of gender, with reference to the first years of life.

In this context of thought, *gender* coincides with the acting and carrying out of behaviour that expresses and represents identity in role, in relation to body changes, interaction and conversation. The theory of *gender performance* (widespread in ethnomethodological sociology, influenced by symbolic interactionist sociology[62]) considers that *gender* falls into the dimension of 'doing', as it is not the reflection of traits inherent to individuals, but the product of social interaction. The same sexual identity or assignment of sex (male or female) depends on acting: acting determines gender, both as role and as identity. Functionalists[63] argue that diversity in the evolution of men and women depends on the different need to achieve the complementary functions essential for survival. Similarly, sociobiologists[64] ascribe the different behaviour of men and women to the different reproductive strategies that have evolved to ensure survival.

The theory of gender schema[65] (similar to the social learning theory, social cognitive theory, cognitive developmental theory) focuses attention on cognitive organisation in the context of socialisation. This theory postulates that children learn and acquire the roles of men and women to varying degrees from culture and society: they internalise this knowledge as a pattern of gender that becomes the core of gender identity that interacts with individual experiences and is reinforced by the mechanism of reward/punishment received based on behaviour. The interaction between the pattern of gender and experiences allows the construction of *gender* identity and the development of traits and behaviour in a consistent manner.[66]

---

[61] H.M. LIPS, *Sex and Gender: an Introduction,* Mayfield, Mountain View (CA) 2001; R. ALSOP, A. FITZSIMONS, K. LENNON, *Theorizing Gender*, Polity, Cambridge 2005.

[62] The theory of symbolic interactionism interprets social interaction as symbolic interaction, social reality as a product of a discursive interaction between individuals and gender as a representation that is produced by the interaction (gender displays).

[63] A.A. SHIELDS, *Functionalism, Darwinism, and the Psychology of Women: a Study in Social Myth*, "American Psychologist", 1975, 30, pp. 739–754.

[64] D.M. BUSS, *Psychological Sex Differences: Origins through Sexual Selection*, "American Psychologist", 1995, 50, pp. 164–168.

[65] S.L. BEM, *Gender Schema Theory: a Cognitive Account of Sex-Typing*, "Psychological Review", 1981, 88, pp. 354–364; ID., *The Lenses of Gender: Transforming the Debate on Sexual Inequality*, Yale University Press, New Haven (CT) 1993; A.E. BELL, R.J. STERNBERG (eds.), *The Psychology of Gender*, Guilford Press, New York 1993.

[66] According to these theories, the apparent failure of sex reassignment in cases of anomalies, depend on an incomplete or inadequate socialisation program.

1.2 Sociological Paths

The doing gender theories[67] interpret socialisation as an active process that is not reduced to mere passive internalization of external expectations, but presupposes and involves negotiation and modification. Children do not limit themselves to perception of the gender messages from outside, but they interact with others building their own identity. The 'agents' of gender socialisation are identified as the family, communication, overall social expectations. The family is the primary source of socialisation as it is the first institution children enter into. From the moment they are born (and even before birth, with the possibility of identifying sex prenatally) parents begin to treat children in different ways, addressing them with specific language, dressing them in certain colours (with the symbolic value that helps others to interact with them), buying specific toys. Family communication is a further source of socialisation. It distinguishes a particular way of communicating, more emotionally for females and more rationally and action directed for males. Different social expectations reinforce gender identification, induced by the family: females are expected to be more docile and calm and males more turbulent and competitive. The 'agents of socialisation' encourage the development of traits and behaviour directly or indirectly.

The theory of social role[68] explains the development of gender in relation to society, ascribing the root of role production to social 'stereotypes'. 'Gender stereotypes' are the common beliefs about people based on belonging to social categories. They vary according to physical characteristics (active in men, passive in women), psychological traits (aggressive, and competitive in men, subordinate and cooperative in women), behaviour (oriented to justice in men, oriented to care in women) and to tasks/functions (participation in public life for men as regards the economy and political power; the private domestic sphere for women).[69] A distinction is made between 'communal role' characterised by care and emotional expression, generally associated with the domestic role and women and that of the 'agentic role' characterised by assertiveness and independence, generally connected with public activities and men.

---

[67] C. WEST, D.H. ZIMMERMAN, *Doing Gender*, "Gender & Society", 1987, 1, pp. 125-151; S. FENSTERMAKER, C. WEST (eds.), *Doing Gender, Doing Difference: Inequality, Power, and Institutional Change*, Routledge, New York 2002.

[68] A.H. EAGLY, *Sex Differences in Social Behavior: a Social Role Interpretation*, Erlbaum, Hillsdale (N.J.) 1987; A.H. EAGLY, W. WOOD, *The Origins of Sex Differences in Human Behaviour: Evolved Dispositions versus Social Roles*, "American Psychologist", 1999, 54, pp. 408–423.

[69] K. DEAUX, L.L. LEWIS, *Assessment of Gender Stereotypes: Methodology and Components*, "Psychological Documents", 1983, 13, p. 25.

1.2.2 Gender as a Social Construction

A systematic critique of essentialism comes from social constructionism,[70] a theory developed in the field of sociology, which has had a major impact in the philosophical debate on gender.[71] Social constructionism is detached from biological essentialism (that recognises identity in essence) as well as from social essentialism (fixing single identity on a social level) and is placed in an intermediate position between pre-modern essentialism and post-modern deconstructionism.

'Constructionism' refers to 'constructivism'. Costrutivism is a predominantly philosophical and epistemological theory according to which it is not possible to objectively represent reality, given that the sphere of our experience is the result of our constructive activity. Nothing exists in itself, regardless of the person who brings it into being.[72] Constructionism is a sociological theory that applies the constructivist theory to society, believing that society is the construction process through which people constantly create not by means of their being, but by means of their acting and interacting, a common and shared reality, experienced as objective. This is the broad nurture theory that, along the lines of narrow nurture, widens the reference of socialisation from the agents of socialisation to social structures in a broad sense, to language and to culture. In this context, gender is considered not only the product of socialisation, but a socio-historical and cultural variable. This theory does not investigate what people 'are', but what they 'do' together as part of the social relations in specific historical and cultural contexts.

The key concepts of the constructionist theory are identified in the three phases of the process which, through action and interaction, allow subjective meanings to be transformed into objective facts and to 'construct' socially the reality, subsequently perceived as natural. The first phase is 'externalisation': it is the moment in which the agents, through their activities, create the social dimensions. Then 'objectification': it is the phase in which individuals, through thought and language, objectivise reality as orderly and preordained, independent of the individual. The last phase is 'internalisation': it is the stage in which, through socialisation, the order constructed subjectively and intersubjectively is accepted and objectively legitimised.

---

[70] S. JACKSON, *Theorizing Gender and Sexuality*, in S. JACKSON, J. JONES (eds.), *Contemporary Feminist Theories*, New York University Press, New York 1998, pp. 134–137.

[71] V. BURR, *An Introduction to Social Constructionism*, Routledge, London-New York 1995; S. JACKSON, S. SCOTT, *Theorizing Sexuality,* Open University Press, New York 2010. Burr defines *gender* as the social significance assumed by sexual differences. In his opinion, the term refers to the constellation of traits and behaviour that end up being associated with males and females respectively and therefore they are expected within a particular society. In other words, it is a term that refers to the concepts of masculinity and femininity and their differences, whether real or alleged. In this sense, sex, a natural element, becomes the anchor on which to create a cultural category, gender.

[72] The perspective seems to recall G. Berkeley's *esse est percipi*.

This theory has contributed to the social elaboration of gender. Starting from the not disputed fact that there are two sexes (man and woman) or sexed identities, the gender category refers to the social process or socialisation (gendering process), but also to the product of this process, which divides people in society into male and female. In this sense, gender is not rooted into gendered beings, but in society (gendered society). Social constructionism affirms that the source of gender is not nature, but history and human action/interactions.[73] Gender is no longer considered as a constitutive element of natural being or inherent essence, but it becomes a quality of social relationship.[74] Gender becomes, therefore, the construction of femininity and masculinity: it is an external creation, influenced by society and determined by culture.

The process of socialisation, in this perspective, is constituted by the widespread association repeated in time between one sex (male/female) and certain social actions/practices (roles, responsibilities, expectations). The description or acknowledgment of such a process leads to the observation that women have a predominantly private role and men a predominantly public role. This determines the association of the female with the reproductive and domestic role and the male with the economic and political role. The distinction becomes and can become social opposition of the sexes or genders. The opposition means that belonging to one sex carries with it, on the historical-social level, the possession of certain characteristics that are supposed to be conflicting: to be a man means not being a woman and not assuming the role of women and vice versa. Hierarchicalisation arises (or may arise) from opposition: in this sense, hierarchy does not come from natural distinction, but from the social construction associated with the natural distinction, insofar as society privileges one category, placing it in a position of superiority or exclusivity, and devaluing the other. Constructionism believes that people are not marginalised because different with respect to sex, but different because marginalised in relation to gender.

Social constructionism marks a transition compared to previous theorisation. It does not stop at the description of the social emergence of gender, but focuses attention on power relations between gender roles. The emphasis on gender in this context is misleading, if this further aspect below is not understood. The theories of this perspective point out, in the socio-historical context, the emergence of models of gender identity/difference that devalue women and the female role. But the premise of the theory is that men and women can occupy both spaces or ways of life: women can participate in public life, and men in private life, it being a problem of gender or social role, and not of biological sex. In this sense, social constructionism proposes new models that revalue women with respect to men, believing that social status is changeable, deconstructable and re-constructable.

---

[73] Cultural differences are used to support this perspective. J. ARCHER, B. LLOYD, *Sex and Gender*, Cambridge University Press, New York 1985.

[74] H.S. BOHAN, *Regarding Gender: Essentialism, Constructionism, and Feminist Psychology*, in M. M. GERGEN, S. N. DAVIS (eds.), *Toward a New Psychology of Gender*, Routledge, New York 1997.

Subordination and oppression are 'unnatural' in as much as they are not rooted in nature, but conveyed by society and culture: they are built, that is, produced and created, through expectations and actions.[75]

It is a theory which, although critical of essentialism, does not absolutely oppose it. It is a theory that detaches itself from essentialism, as it states that the man/woman differentiation is also a social process, not only the direct expression of nature; moreover, it criticises the overlapping of sex and gender, and introduces a contrast between sex, the term fixes identity statically to nature and gender, which flexibly indicates a process. But at the same time, this theory does not oppose 'in principle' the two terms, but rather it detects 'in fact' the contrast, highlighting the strong interaction in the context of the phenomenological interconnection between nature and society.[76] On this basis, constructionism believes that ignorance of this interaction presupposes a distorted way of understanding the body (as inert matter) and society (as not influential on nature). The interconnection does not preclude the possible change in the relationship between nature/society (and therefore also sex/gender), insofar as they affect power relations.

This theory is not opposed to identity categories (as in post-modern deconstructionism), but it criticises this approach as essentialist, with fixed, eternal and unchanging content. Sexual identities (men and women) do not have pre-determined essence, but neither are they elusive because of their instability. They have variable content that changes in society and history, as part of a material process. Compared to essentialism, social constructionism recognises that it is not possible to entirely escape from the notion of identity or essence by talking of sex and gender:[77] the use of simple and homogeneous categories of identity is at least strategically necessary. The criticism of essentialism arises in general, believing that the sexual phenomenon (identity, acts and sexuality) is not reducible to a fundamental nucleus of intrinsic truth.

1.2.3 Gender as a Cultural Construction

The theorisation of gender as cultural construction is along the same lines. In this area also there is criticism of the essentialist claim to explain and biologically understand sexual phenomena in a universal way. An innate, profound and unchanging character of sex "uncontaminated by cultural influences"[78] is believed

---

[75] J. LORBER, *Paradoxes of Gender*, Yale University Press, New Haven (CT) 1994.

[76] J. SCOTT, *Some Reflections on Gender and Politics*, in M.M. FERREE, J. LORBER, B.B. BESS (eds.), *Revisioning Gender*, Sage-Thousand Oaks, CA London 1999.

[77] D. FUSS, *Essentially Speaking: Feminism, Nature and Difference*, Routledge, New York–London 1989, p. 9 and p. 18.

[78] S. JACKSON, S. SCOTT, *Sexual Skirmishes and Feminist Factions: Twenty-five Years of Debate on Women and Sexuality*, in S. JACKSON, S. SCOTT (eds.), *Feminism and Sexuality: a Reader*, Edinburgh University Press, Edinburgh 1996, p. 11.

to be inexistant and unknowable. The thematisation of gender as cultural construction is delineated by following diverse paths: gender as a cultural construction of sex and as a cultural construction of sexuality.[79]

Ann Oakley[80] notes that *gender* is a "matter of culture", as it refers to the cultural classification of masculine and feminine as opposed to sex, that biologically distinguishes male from female. The constancy of sex and the variability of gender is revealed: this proves that biology has a minimal role in the development of gender identity and that gender is not a direct, mechanical and automatic product of sex. The author maintains that cultural learning far exceeds biological determination, referring also to studies of hermaphroditism as evidence of the irrelevance of biology and the relevance, and perhaps also the 'power', of culture.

Gayle Rubin[81] offers an elaborate analysis, in the context of cultural anthropology, of the question recalling the historical-dialectical method of F. Engels, the anthropological and cultural contributions of C. Lévi-Strauss and the psychoanalysis of S. Freud and J. Lacan. The author identifies in the sex/gender distinction the "most effective" conceptual pair to express the male/female relationship: sex indicates the natural difference that in itself does not produce different social roles and gender properly indicates the roles produced by culture and the socio-historical context. Gender is defined as "socially imposed division of the sexes", but also as "the product of the social relations of sexuality". The "sex/gender system" refers to the series of measures by which biological sex and sexuality are configured on a social level, with reference to the organisation of human sexual relations, or "institutional forms of sexuality" through the structure of kinship and marriage. In this perspective the connection between sex and sexuality[82] becomes increasingly explicit.

The author denies the necessary dependence on sex/gender and the determination of sex with respect to gender. On the contrary, she believes that the difference in roles is produced by culture, independently of the sexual difference. This thesis is in line—according to Rubin—with the claims made by Engels who considers the difference between men and women in social roles defined by the productive sphere of the 'economic system' on the reproductive sphere of the 'sexual system'. It is also similar to the theory of Lévi-Strauss, who tracks in the systems of kinship the rule of exchange of women among men as an imposition of

---

[79] R.W. CONNELL, *Gender*, Polity Press, Cambridge 2002.

[80] A. OAKLEY, *Sex, Gender and Society*, Martin Robertson, Oxford 1972.

[81] Cf. G. RUBIN, *The Traffic in Women: Notes on the "Political Economy" of Sex*, in E. LEWIN (ed.), *Feminist Anthropology. A Reader*, Blackwell, Oxford 2006, p. 87 and ff. A subsequent re-elaboration of the theory in G. RUBIN, *Sexual Traffic* (interview with Judith Butler), "Differences: a Journal of Feminist Cultural Studies", 1994, 6, 2/3, pp. 62–99. Cf. J.W. SCOTT, *Gender: a Useful Category of Historical Analysis*, "The American Historical Review", 1986, 91, 5, pp. 1053–1075.

[82] G. RUBIN, *Thinking Sex: Notes for a Radical Theory of the Politics of Sexuality*, in C.S. VANCE (ed.), *Pleasure and Danger: Exploring Female Sexuality*, Routledge & Kegan Paul, New York 1984, p. 277.

culture on matters of procreation that produce sexual division. And finally, it corresponds to the description of Freud and Lacan of the mechanisms through which children take on the rules regarding sex and gender, from the pre-Oedipal phase where there is lack of sexual distinction or bisexuality at the Oedipal phase that produces sexual division.[83] In these processes, described and structured in different ways, there emerges a common element: the economic, cultural and social factors produce sexual division, not in an equal way but in an asymmetrical way.

According to Rubin, the "sex/gender system" has—in recent Western societies—led prevalently to the dominion of men: heterosexual marriage and the division of labor according to sex have led to attribution of the maternal-domestic role to women and of the public role to men. Sexual asymmetry has determined social asymmetry (presumed natural) and hierarchy between "those exchanging" (men) and "those being exchanged" (women), from which the oppression of women, and, at the same time, the perception of "compulsory heterosexuality" are contingent. The analysis of gender demonstrates that the division of the sexes is socially imposed, that the oppression of women does not concern the biological sphere but rather the social system and that the same root of women's oppression also causes homosexual oppression. According to Rubin gender is not only the "identification with one sex, but also the obligation to direct sexual desire toward the opposite sex".[84] In this sense there should be denaturalisation of the subordination of women/men, as well as the heterosexual choice. The author reconstructs a pyramid of sexual relations, revealing how cultural priority is given to those that are 'heterosexual, married, monogamous, reproductive, and non-commercial' and how in contrast, those that are 'homosexual, not married, promiscuous, non-monogamous not reproductive, and commercial' are marginal and considered inferior.

The sex/gender system is a series of ways of dealing with gender identity and sexuality and coincides with the cultural and social organisation of gender, as a determinant structure subject to transformation and development in space and time. This system represents the series of strategies by which the biological material of sexuality and procreation is shaped by human intervention. It is a kind of measure through which society transforms sexual biological instinct in human sexual activity in relation to modes of reproduction and patriarchy. Rubin identifies, through an empirical, anthropological and cultural investigation of the organisation of family and kinship the heart of the sex/gender system, therefore the structure of society. These roles are related to cultural appertainance, consequently, they are variable within the different geographical areas and historical periods.

---

[83] The author distinguishes between a Freudian biological interpretation and Lacan's unbiological/simbolic interpretation.

[84] «Gender is not only an identification with one sex: it also entails that sexual desire be directed toward the other sex», G. RUBIN, *The Traffic in Women*, cit., p. 95.

In the context of her cultural, anthropological and psychoanalytical analysis, the author shows how natural biological data can be transformed—on a social, historical, and cultural level—in a binary system both symmetrically equal (in which men and women occupy the same position) as well as asymmetrically hierarchical (in which the male occupies a privileged position compared to the female). In this sense, the author highlights that what feminism has to fight—so that women can reach a position of equality to men—is not the difference of sex, but the difference of gender. Gender needs to be eliminated, sex liberated from the roles imposed by gender and, on this basis, a gender needs to be built that puts men and women on an equal position.[85] One method, in her opinion, is through the abolition of the division of gender roles and through the expansion of care to the father alongside the mother: the care of both parents from birth would take away the root causes of the Oedipus and Electra complex, which give rise to gender roles.

It should be noted that Oakley and Rubin emphasize the cultural construction of gender but assume without questioning the biological basis of sex on which the distinction is grounded: in the case of Oakley the anatomical sexual difference, in the case of Rubin procreative sexual activity.[86] Alongside the reflections of Oakley and Rubin, there are many studies of cultural anthropology that intersect with the gender category, putting in evidence the presence of past but also present societies that accepted the 'third sex', 'third gender' or 'neutral gender'[87], unlike the western culture.[88] Cultural anthropology, on a descriptive level, brings elements to show that what is 'abnormal' in one culture may be 'normal' in another culture, introducing provocative reflection on the category of gender from a cultural standpoint.

---

[85] «Sex/gender system (...) is a neutral term which refers to the domain and indicates that oppression is not inevitable in that domain, but is the product of the specific social relations which organize it» (G. RUBIN, *The Traffic in Women*, cit., p. 91). The author criticises the excesses of anti-machoist feminism.

[86] S. JACKSON, *Theorizing Gender and Sexuality*, in S. JACKSON, J. JONES (eds.), *Contemporary Feminist Theories*, Edinburgh University Press, Edinburgh 1998, pp. 131-146, in particular see p. 134.

[87] Among which, those who have physical anomalies are cited: the 'Berdache' among the indigenous peoples of North and South America (but also in Oceania, Siberia, Asia and Africa) or individuals with 'two spirits', male and female, thought of as having supernatural powers; the 'hijras' in India a special caste recognised as neither male nor female; the 'Khanith' in Islamic culture; the 'turnim man' in New Guinea and 'guevodoces' in the Dominican Republic. In Thailand 'pheet' refers to a category of individuals with multiple gender. Among those that do not correspond to traditional social roles; the 'acault' in Burma (socially recognised as a male but they live as females); 'faa fa'fini' (Samoa), 'fakaleiti' (Tonga) and 'mahu' (Hawaii and Tahiti), men with feminine identity and behavior; 'shamans' of mixed sex, with non-masculine men and non-feminine women.

[88] G. HERDT, *Third Sex, Third Gender: Beyond Sexual Dimorphism in Culture and History*, Basic Books, New York 1994.

1.3 Philosophical Paths of Feminism

1.3.1 From Equality/Difference to the Question of Sex/Gender

The theory of social constructionism is elaborated within the sphere of sociological and cultural anthropology, in close connection to some theories of feminism. In feminist philosophy[89] among the concepts introduced in the context of the debate on the relationship between men/women one frequently finds use of the *gender* category, especially starting from the 70's, but also previously.[90]

As known, the core concept of feminism is identification—within the context of human relationships between males and females—of the root of the assumption of male superiority in relation to the female that makes women marginal subjects. In short, it is the search for the origin of the phenomenon of sexual discrimination, generally referred to as 'sexism' in the sense of patriarchal androcentrism.[91] It is in this context that some feminist theories fit into the sex/gender debate,[92] applying the conceptual distinction specifically to the so-called feminist issue.

Feminism thematises the gender category as distinct from sex in the analysis of the man/woman relationship (only marginally in relation to sexuality). The idea that develops with increasing conviction in feminism is that gender does not coincide with sex. Sex is how we are born: therefore, it is—indisputably—a natural element or a biological fact. Gender is how we become: therefore not, at least entirely and exclusively, determined by biology. Feminist perspectives affirm that what we become does not coincide with what we are and how we are born. It is precisely on the basis of the thematisation of the distinction and separation of sex/gender that a part of feminism thematises the possibility that the male/female hierarchy, found in fact historically and socially, is overturnable. The conceptual pair sex/gender is thematised first implicitly, then explicitly in diverse ways within feminist philosophy, in the various liberal, socialist, and radical theories.

Early feminism focuses on the categories of equality/difference, and only implicitly on gender. In this context, the sexual difference of men/women is

---

[89] For a reconstruction of the feminist debate within the context of the sex/gender opposition see A. STONE, *An Introduction to Feminist Philosophy*, Polity, Cambridge-Malden (MA) 2007.

[90] Some authors explicitly deny that feminism has originally developed the category of *gender* as opposed to *sex* (cf. D. THOMPSON, *The Sex/Gender Distinction: a Reconsideration*, "Australian Feminist Studies", 1989, 10, p. 23). Moreover, it is an infrequently used category with this meaning in feminism. Some, however, believe that the category was coined by Anglophone feminism (cf. W.C. HARRISON, J. HOOD-WILLIAMS, *Beyond Sex and Gender*, Sage, London 2002, p. 25).

[91] With reference to the vast quantity of literature one is restricted to mention only: R. TONG, *Feminist Thought: a More Comprehensive Introduction*, Allen and Uniwin, Sidney 1998; C. BEASLEY, *What is Feminism? An Introduction to Feminist Theory*, Sage, London 1999.

[92] A. STONE, *An Introduction to Feminist Philosophy*, cit., p. 3; S. POCHA, *Feminism and Gender*, in S. GAMBLE (ed.), *The Routledge Companion to Feminism and Postfeminism*, Routledge, London 2001, pp. 55–65.

considered irrelevant, in a perspective of egalitarian assimilation of man. The reason for the oppression of women is found in society (therefore in gender) and not in the condition of sex. Equality becomes an absolute paradigm, with the consequent annulment of female specificity in configuration of a model without differences.

Subsequently the focus shifts explicitly on the categories of sex/gender.[93] It is outlined in gender feminism as opposed to the feminism of equality.[94] It is precisely on sexual difference that philosophical debate concentrates in this area. The sexual condition of women—understood as the anatomy of the female body and reproductive function in the gestational sense (pregnancy, childbirth, breastfeeding)—is considered to be the root of women's inferiority in relation to men, and their condition of subjection. Women, because of their biological condition (i.e. sex) have acquired a private, domestic and caring role, which constitutes an obstacle to participation in public, social, political and economic life to which men have access. The lack of conceptual distinction and the factual connection of sex/gender (i.e. the consideration of sex as a necessary and sufficient cause of gender) has produced the subordination of women. Feminism becomes aware of the fact that it is sex that determines gender (according to the 'anatomy as destiny' thesis), women are inevitably caged and forced into a biological condition of subservience to men and to society, relegated to a domestic and caring role.

But feminism reacts to the disadvantaged condition that has been historically and socially attributed to women.[95] The inferiority of the role is not the inevitable result of the biological difference in relation to men, but is something that must and should be changed.[96] Through thematisation of the distinction/separation of *sex/gender,* feminism intends to liberate women from marginalization and make them regain a position of equality, in accordance with some philosophical lines: the demonstration of the irrelevance of sex for gender (what we 'are', is not important but what we 'become' is, regardless of birth) and the consideration of gender as a social construction, not determined by nature, but structured by society and culture. Even the use of new technologies (contraception, sterilisation, abortion and reproductive technologies)—separating sex from procreation—allow women to overcome the disadvantage determined by their biological condition and overcome its limitations.

The gender category is greatly used in this sense in the context of feminism. Sometimes simply and perhaps even naïvely as a synonym for sex, at other times it is consciously thematised as a meta-biological category that allows the theorising

---

[93] The paths outlined do not follow a strictly historical reconstruction, instead, they identify conceptual itineraries.

[94] C.H. SOMMERS, *Who Stole Feminism?*, Simon & Schuster, New York 1997.

[95] Within the context of *gender* there are theories dealing with the political aspect (the realisation of equality and individual self-determination), the historical-social aspect (justification of the end of the role of the female in Western societies) and the philosophical aspect (the relationship between human beings and nature).

[96] This is the nucleus of feminist thought identified by V. BRYSON, *Feminist Political Theory: an Introduction*, Macmillan, Basingstoke 1992, p. 192.

of a path for women's liberation. The use of the term is in some way convenient for 'women's studies' (but also for 'men's studies').[97] It opens new theoretical paths from biological fixity to social malleability. There are not only linguistic reasons for the choice of the term, but also a precise political and social theory. Gender gives weight to the social construction of sexual inequality, to what is not biologically given in the disparity between men/women.[98] In this direction, even in feminism (in parallel and contextually to psychosexology, psychoanalysis, sociology and cultural anthropology) a critique of biological determinism and essentialism emerges in a gradual and articulated manner: beginning weakly, and later becoming increasingly strong and extreme.

1.3.2 Women are Like Men: Oppression as a Matter of Gender

The birth of feminist thought in the late 1700s and early 1800s (in 1792, the year of publication of *A Vindication of the Rights of Women* by Mary Wollstonecraft[99] or in 1791 with the *Déclaration des droits de la femme et de la citoyenne* by Olympe de Gouges)[100] was connected to the female disquiet, with women being denied space in all areas of public life.

Wollstonecraft can be considered an anticipator of the sex/gender debate-Although she did not use these categories in such an explicitly opposite way, she began to develop a perspective that shows its importance.[101] The author is aware that the oppression of women is not a fact of nature but a social fact, that is, it does not depend on internal factors, such as biological condition, but on external factors, such as education and social organisation. In other words, it is a matter of gender, not sex. Education and cultural formation allowed only for males, keep women "far from the truth" and make them "slaves of opinion": equal access to education (therefore a change in social conditions) is considered essential for appropriate entry into society and for recognition of equal dignity and equal rights.[102] The starting point is the recognition of women as "rational creatures", a prerequisite in order to build a "rational friendship" with men in the place of "servile obedience". De Gouge, in the same year, aims to combat sexist

---

[97] M. LIBERTIN, *The Politics of Women's Studies and Men's Studies*, "Hypatia", 1987, 2, pp. 143–152.

[98] This is the path taken in Anglo-American literature, but not however by Italian and French feminism.

[99] M. WOLLSTONECRAFT, *A Vindication of the Rights of Woman* (1792), *A Vindication of the Rights of Women and a Vindication of the Rights of Men*, Oxford University Press, Oxford 2009.

[100] O. DE GOUGE, *Déclaration des droits de la femme et de la citoyenne* (1791).

[101] A. STONE, *An Introduction to Feminist Philosophy*, cit., p. 11.

[102] It must be remembered that the author is addressing middle-class educated women in her opinion closer to the natural state, not aristocratic women engaged in pleasing men or women of the working classes, whose social elevation is prevented by oppression.

1.3 Philosophical Paths of Feminism

oppression in order to reaffirm the "sacred and inalienable rights of the woman" after "ignorance, neglect, and contempt". She affirms that "woman is born free and lives equal to man in her right", appealing to the concept of "equal dignity". This is the conceptual approach within which the "first wave of feminism"[103] (1848-1918) is structured, with its focus on emancipation, in the sense of enfranchisement and liberation of nature from the oppression of society.

Equality feminism is divided into two main strands: liberal and socialist.[104] These orientations, despite their differences in argumentation, share the emancipationist ideal. A movement of thought was born which is also a political movement, by which women make their voices heard as well as the strength of their ideas and proposals.

Harriet Taylor in the essay *The Emancipation of Women* (1851) and John Stuart Mill in *The Subjection of Women* (1869),[105] in the context of liberal feminism, refute the alleged natural inferiority of women, claiming that every human being is by nature rational and autonomous morally. The attempt is to overcome the subjection of women due to education, history and culture so that women can regain the natural rights denied and not recognised by society. Taylor insists in particular on education, employment, political participation, believing that women can achieve freedom through liberation from care of the family. Mill affirms that women, although physically weaker than men, should not be subjugated to them: the physical difference does not justify the social subordination, that is a sort of slavery. A particular form of slavery, that of women: the enslavement of women in the family, exercised not through strength, but with affection, which prevents collective rebellion. In this sense, women educated constantly to the duty of self-denial, must revindicate equality to men in political rights by appealing to rational capacities. It is the natural equality of the rights of every human being regardless of sex that accounts for the obligation of equal treatment in education, economic management, employment and voting.[106]

Marxist and socialist thought,[107] even though in a different theoretical perspective, share with liberal feminism, the revindication of the emancipation of women, through access to employment and the public sphere. This theory frames the issue of the

---

[103] The word appears only in 1895, but the movement goes back to a few decades earlier.

[104] The 'first wave' of feminism refers to a period between the end of 1700s, half of the 1800s until the period between the world wars (1848-1918). The chronological distinction is problematic, since in the early decades of the twentieth century reflections began to glide from emancipation to pacifism, the problems of sexuality, the value of female experience.

[105] J.S. MILL, H. TAYLOR, *Essays on Sexual Equality*, University of Chicago Press, Chicago 1970.

[106] Also worth mentioning is the declaration of the rights of women proposed by E.C. Stanton (1815-1902) that moves from the truth, believed to be self-evident "that all men and women are created equal" and therefore have the inalienable right to equality.

[107] If liberal feminism developed mainly in England and in the U.S. (given the greater weight of political liberalism compared to Europe), after the second world war in European countries, with the development of welfare state systems, it was the socialist feminists, or the left in general, that conveyed the revindications of women.

problem of women's status in the context of class inequalities arising from the capitalist economic system. Even in this perspective the reasons for the oppression of women are not identified in nature, but in society. Therefore, even the prospects for improvement of the status of women are found in social change, specifically in the economic conditions of women, through their integration into the working class fighting for recognition of equal access to employment. Socialist feminism (as opposed to liberal feminism, which relies on free competition of the logic of the market) calls for State intervention in the sphere of social policies to ensure the conditions that enable women to participate in employment and public life, to make real and effective the rights gained in terms of principles.[108] It is the perspective that believes that through the communist revolution in a socialist society all forms of subordination will disappear, along with those of the proletarians in relation to capitalists, and also those of women in relation to men. The interests of women are therefore proposed as an ally of the proletarians for the revolution of socialism.

Friedrich Engels in the essay *Der Ursprung der Familie, des Privateigenthums und des Staats* (1884)[109] reconstructs anthropologically the original state of sexual promiscuity (in which all males had sexual relations with all females, regardless of age and kinship) that characterised society before the formation of the monogamous family. The author highlights that women in the prehistory of humanity were not in a subordinate position: indeed they were venerated even religiously as a symbol of fertility. In the social transformation of work (from hunting and gathering, to farming, agriculture and war), the male acquires a primary role as head of the family, owner of territory, livestock, slaves, and even women. Engels believes that the monogamous family was born in Greek and Roman civilisations with the institution of private property: in this context sexual relationships were transformed (the first exclusion regarded the sexual relations of mothers-fathers with their sons-daughters, then between consanguineous brothers-sisters) in the transition from 'matriarchy' (a state of equality, if not of female superiority) to 'patriarchy' (a state of male superiority). The transition from prehistory to history marks the birth of 'women's enslavement': monogamous marriage is considered men's dominion over women. The socialist revolution is proposed as a condition for the liberation of all women (not only those of the proletariat) through the change of social conditions (i.e. gender), the abolition of private property and the establishment of common property. The care and education of children becomes a public affair.

In striving for the pursuit of the equality of women to men (women 'as' men),[110] in the context of liberal feminism and socialist feminism, there is thematisation of

---

[108] This is the thesis advanced by male thinkers (F. Engels, A. Bebel) and female thinkers (A. Kollontaj, K. Zetkin), even anarchic thinkers (E. Goldman).

[109] F. ENGELS, *Der Ursprung der Familie, des Privateigenthums und des Staats* (1884), English translation, *The Origin of the Family, Private Property and the State*, Penguin Classics, London 2010.

[110] The most important methods used for this purpose were the institutional struggle, law and organised mass action for equal opportunities. Feminism has also taken on different characteristics depending on the social, legal and political system in which it has spread.

the idea that what should be changed is not nature, considered equal in men and women, but society, the source of inequality. The modification of social conditions, allowing access to education and employment for women, provides the guarantee of equal rights. Gender begins to be, even though still implicitly, a reference point in the search for modification of the female social role regardless of natural condition.

1.3.3 Rethinking: the Second Sex Questions Nature and Culture

In the context of feminist reflection (1918–1968) there are various lines of rethinking of the relationship between equality/difference, which is intertwined in many respects with the sex/gender question. In this context, despite the heterogeneity of the reflections, a common element is perceived: the identification of sex (corresponding to nature) of the reasons for the inferiority of women and the search for a modification of gender in society and culture.

Simone de Beauvoir[111] in the volume *Le deuxième sex* (1949) addresses the issue of the condition of subordination of women, seeking the causes through a detailed analysis in biological, psychoanalytical, historical, ethnographic and mythological terms. This analysis is placed in a philosophical horizon that comes from a synthesis of existentialism and Hegelianism. The existentialist assumption taken up by the philosophy of Sartre, coincides with the thesis: existence precedes essence. It is a materialist vision which opposed to essentialism affirms the antecedence and exclusivity of existence, that is, what man is in his concrete reality. It is a nominalist anti-metaphysical view that believes that being human is an abstract concept, as only real and concrete individuals exist in the specific.

In this context, the author believes that «one is not born a woman, but becomes one». According to the author every human being (man or woman) is self-sufficient and makes himself/herself. Every man is the result of free acts, creating himself in time. He is able to choose from two paths: the path of "transcendence", that is the active transformation of the world (for those who live 'for themselves') and the path of "immanence", that is passive acceptance of things as they are (for those who live 'in themselves'). De Beauvoir applies these categories to the understanding of the female condition: a woman exists as she becomes, she projects herself into the world, transcending her immanence[112] through the exercise of conscience and liberty. But women are incapable of transcending themselves: they have been historically confined and "imprisoned" to remain in the immanence of the body, destined for procreation, motherhood, and domestic work (defined as the "trap of motherhood"), in the passivity and objectivity that chain them to a state of subordination. Women have found themselves in the condition of being "Other" in

---

[111] S. DE BEAUVOIR, *Le deuxième sexe*, Gallimard, Paris 1949.

[112] Transcendence not in the spiritual but in the materialistic sense: transcendent in the sense that it differs from the animal, but not because it is part of the spirituality of essence.

relation to men by nature; but women have also chosen to be "Other" in the social context.[113] Although influenced by their biological state, they have not been forced to accept this inferior status, for which they are also "accomplices". "No biological, psychological, economic destiny defines the face that the human female assumes in the heart of society". The author locates in "history and civilisation as a whole" the cause of the female condition, as well as biological condition. In a sense, in her view, sex and gender are the causes of the hierarchical order of the inferiority of women to men, of women's condition in "second sex", from which they must break free to become equal to men.

A woman is not "a fixed reality", but a "becoming". She is not born as woman, but she has become one, because of internal biological and psychological conditions and external social and historical conditions. But she can also cease to be one, choosing to become "other" (in lower case), placing herself in a position of equality to men, without conflict. She must from "passive object" without freedom, become an "active subject": she must transcend herself, create culture beyond nature, free herself from the confinement that harnesses her to nature,[114] in the "slavery" of marriage, reproduction and motherhood. She has been pinned to the biological reproductive role and the social domestic role, confined and alienated in immanence, to dependence "in the flesh and in the home", prevented from carrying out her own liberation and transcendence. She has been historically excluded from the dialectic (in the Hegelian sense), i.e. the relational dynamics of recognition for which reciprocity is a requirement. In this sense, a woman need not be or remain a woman, but should "become" a woman, seeking the road for affirmation of her freedom which must "emerge into the light of transcendence". In this sense «one is not born a woman, but becomes one».[115] This is the phrase that gender theories make use of, with a different meaning, but to some extent anticipated by De Beauvoir, in that she considers that "womanity" is socially constructed transcending nature.

Betty Friedan[116] in the volume *The Feminine Mystique* (1969) pursues the same lines, albeit within a different philosophical context, deploring the condition of the feminine mystique, the ideal and idealised condition in which women devoted to home and family are relegated, finding fulfillment through domestic/reproductive family life, renouncing public life. "Mona Lisa's enigmatic smile" represents, in her opinion, the interior crisis of women apparently gratified by marriage and the family, they experience a sensation of emptiness, feeling robbed of their identity, defined socially by the function of being bride, mother, homemaker, and end up feeling "incomplete". On this basis, there is revindication of a public space for

---

[113] According to the author, Man is "the Subject, the Absolute": women seem the only negative "she is the other".

[114] De Beauvoir believes that the word 'female' sounds unpleasant (or even an insult) because it places women in nature and imprisons them to sex. While 'male' is said with pride.

[115] This phrase becomes the reference point of gender theorisation (cf. S. TARRANT, *When Sex became Gender*, Routledge, London 2006).

[116] B. FRIEDAN, *The Feminine Mystique*, Norton, New York 1971.

women, with the same function and role as men in society, in education and employment as in the exercise of power. The "feminine mystique" (proposed to the public even with scientific, psychoanalytical or anthropological legitimacy deemed unfounded by the author) entrenches women in nature which forces her into the "cage" of the family, reproduction, looking after children and the home, from which it is possible to escape only by rejecting this and changing their social role.

Juliet Mitchell[117] in the essay *Women: the Longest Revolution* (1966) critically examines the limitations of the socialist vision in relation to women, focusing on the plight of working women as well as those of the middle class, exploited inside and outside the domestic environment. In her view, the causes of the subordination of women are attributable to production, reproduction, sexuality and the socialization of children. In order to attain the liberation of women it is essential to transform all four elements: production, through the socialist revolution that would eliminate private property and class exploitation;[118] reproduction, separating sexuality from procreation (even with the use of birth control pills); sexuality, by dividing property and marriage (the liberalisation of prostitution and the normalising of homosexuality alongside heterosexuality); the socialisation of children, calling for the shared participation of fathers in the care of the domestic environment and the increase of social services. In this sense the reasons for the inferiority are identified in social condition (therefore *gender*) that must be changed, in parallel to the separation of sexuality from procreation.

1.3.4 The Sexual Revolution: Women Beyond Their Biological Destiny

The sex/gender debate becomes explicit in the context of the 'second wave' of feminism (1968–1980). Radical feminism (also called 'new feminism')[119] looks for a different solution to the female issue, a response that goes to the basis. At the root of the domination of women by men, understood as the domination of all men over all women,[120] there is not only social exclusion and economic exploitation,

---

[117] J. MITCHELL, *Women: the Longest Revolution*, New Left Review, Boston 1966; ID., *Psychoanalysis and Feminism*, Penguin Books, Harmondsworth 1990; ID., *Woman's Estate*, Vintage Books, New York 1973.

[118] The author analyses the compatibility between capitalism and patriarchy as systems of exploitation. The impoverishment of women is a result of the primary division of labor according to sex and the consideration of women in the maternal and domestic sphere (exploitation of women as sex objects, mothers, and educators).

[119] Radical feminism, rightly termed, developed between 1967 and 1975. It is a movement founded by P. Allen and S. Firestone, called 'new social movement' or even 'post-socialism'.

[120] While in the past, women accepted men as allies (think of Mill and Engels), in the manifesto of new feminism, 1969 (Redstocking Group, New York), men are excluded from feminist theorising.

but also and above all the sphere of sexuality. It is the biological and anatomical difference in sex as "immutable destiny" that has determined a difference in gender or in social roles. The sexual and reproductive condition of women forces them into the role of carer and the maternal domestic role that relegates them to an inferior social status in relation to men. In this sense, feminism is opposed to biological and social determinism.[121]

On this basis, radical feminism believes that women's liberation is liberation from the body, extending as far as dissolution of female identity. The destruction of the female model (and therefore the destruction of motherhood, the domestic role, women's attitude and behaviour) is considered the indispensable prerequisite for the construction of a post-model that is not a mere imitation of the male or male assimilation. The objective is not equality as assimilation (believed to be false equality), but equality as liberation from the exploitation of women through "consciousness/self-awareness" of male oppression. Liberation is meant as something different from emancipation. It is a movement that has spread in theoretical and practical terms, in thought and deeds. It is in this perspective that consciousness-raising groups are also established as a form of political activism,[122] the politics of experience and participatory democracy to encourage active participation of the individual under the motto "the personal is political". It is believed that the personal experiences of sexuality, family and motherhood are not only private but also public issues, as they are causes of women's oppression. The birth of 'gender consciousness' means conscious awareness of oppression owing to the sex/gender connection. The history of the relationship between the sexes has been a history of exploitation and domination: liberation must be expressed by means of a revolution first in the domestic and then in the political environment. We must transform not only the public sphere (education, labor, civil and political rights) but also the private one, expanding it to all areas of life. This orientation of thought is particularly prevalent in the U.S. and has put forward the requests for dissemination of methods of contraception, the legalisation of abortion, the establishment of women's counselling centers for sexual problems.

Kate Millett[123] in the volume *Sexual Politics* (1970) identifies 'politics' as a structured relationship of power of a group of people over another group of people and 'sex' as the root of politics, understood as a relationship of domination/subordination. *Sex* then becomes a category with political implications. Patriarchy or patriarchal system is defined as sexual politics, that is, a series of sexist strategies to maintain a system of power and control, that of men over women. Sexual intercourse is considered not an act of pleasure or of procreation, but a 'political fact/act', which establishes and perpetuates male domination over women.

---

[121] In this sense a critique of psychoanalytical theories emerges, including the theory of sexuality that would imply the inferiority of women as an immutable destiny.

[122] Mostly made up of small groups of women, mainly but not exclusively, middle class, white and heterosexual.

[123] K. MILLETT, *Sexual Politics*, University of Illinois Press, Urbana-Chicago 1969.

1.3 Philosophical Paths of Feminism

The 'female gender' is inferior due to the male's interest to keep it in submissiveness: this has led to a loss of women's self-esteem and the reduction of their femininity to acceptance of patriarchal order. Only the destruction of patriarchy can enable a feminist revolution as a 'sexual revolution'. The author, referring explicitly to Stoller,[124] identifies in the splitting of sex/gender the route to this revolution: the separation of sex and gender justifies the split between sexual condition and sexual role. Therefore sexual freedom is guaranteed in the strong sense, that is, women's emancipation and liberation from sexuality.

Shulamith Firestone[125] in the volume *The Dialectic of Sex* (1970) identifies the oppression of women in biological condition (sex) that determines the difference in role as the "tyranny of the biological family". Women conceive, generate, nourish, give care, in a sort of "division of labor" in relation to men: the sexual condition of pregnancy, maternity and care place women in a dimension of weakness. Motherhood is a "reproductive servitude determined by biology". It is therefore nature that puts women in a state of subjection, passivity and dependence, forcing them to seek the help of men, in the family and society. If nature has determined the state of inferiority, it is culture (gender) that can provide release: 'culture' is meant as the transformation of society and roles, as well as the use of the new technologies made available by science. Firestone envisions a society in which scientific and technical progress free women from the "slavery of sexuality and procreation" as liberation from male sexual domination. The author writes: "we can no longer justify the maintenance of a sexual discrimination class by invoking its origins in Nature". Firestone believes it essential to develop a systematic, comprehensive and scientific ideology as an alternative to Marxism. As part of a materialistic and economic interpretation of history, the author introduces the 'dialectic of sex' instead of class struggle, deeming it indispensable to build a new historical materialism. The dialectic of sex constitutes the historical, social and economic infrastructure that determines the superstructure of ideologies, like religion, ethics and culture. This interpretation of reality allows the passage from 'utopian feminism' to 'scientific feminism' that must interpret the world in order to transform it.

Firestone believes that the main objective of the revolution is the family: women's revolution must come about through their taking control of their bodies, their fertility and the 'means of reproduction' (the pill, abortion, reproductive technologies), similar to the revolution of the proletariat that wanted to control the 'means of production'. The first requirement is the separation of sexuality from reproduction, extension of contraceptive methods for free polymorphic sexuality, seen as fun and games. In her view, sexuality should not have a pro-creative purpose, but rather a re-creative one. A further step should be the abolition of the biological family, that is the cause of the existence of the incest taboo, the origin of sexual repression perceived from childhood: the abolition of the biological family would

---

[124] The author refers to cases of intersex to show the splitting of *sex/gender*.

[125] S. FIRESTONE, *The Dialectic of Sex. The Case for Feminist Revolution*, William Morrow and Company, New York 1970.

enable liberation from the inhibition of pleasure instincts and impulses, instituting the 'society of Eros' with the principle of pleasure as its focal point. Firestone, like Millett, finds an analogy between the myth of femininity and that of childhood: even childhood is a cultural construction that has to be sexually liberated, against the culture of protection. In her opinion, sexual revolution involves cancellation of the distinctions of sex in relation to age (extending sexual liberation beyond adults, to children), number (increasing bonds to more than two people), marital status (married and umnarried), family ties (allowing even incest), gender (considering heterosexuality equivalent to homosexuality).[126] Maternity and children would only be freely choosen by women, and the care of children would be socialized, shared by women and men in an undifferentiated way through social services.[127]

1.3.5 Lesbian Separatism

On an historical and social level as well as a theroetical one, the feminist criticism of sex as determining the inferiority of women in relation to men, develops parallel to the criticism of heterosexuality as a social institution and norm, within the sphere of lesbian separatism, anticipating the sex/gender/sexuality debate.[128] Intrasexual feminism, or lesbian separatism, (as opposed to heterosexual feminism, considered patriarchal) leads to the formation of only women communities. Heterosexual oriented feminism, anti-sexist and anti-patriarchal, is divided from lesbian feminism, which claims the right to express and declare one's sexual orientation and not just relegate it to the private sphere. In this context, the gender category begins also to refer to sexual orientation, as a free sexual choice dictated by desire and impulse.[129]

Adrienne Rich[130] does not theorise the lesbianism of non-women/non-men, but of lesbian identities. In her view, the categories of heterosexuality and homosexuality need to disappear in the fight against the patriarchal system that has institutionalised the heterosexual family as the norm. It introduces the idea that sexism and hetero-sexism, or hetero-normativity (compulsory heterosexuality) as

---

[126] Lesbian feminism believes that marriage is institutionalisation of the normativity of heterosexuality.

[127] M. DALY, *Gyn/Ecology. The Metaethics of Radical Feminism*, The Women's Press Ltd., London 1979. The author focuses on the links between the patriarchal system and Judeo-Christian religious tradition, believing that it has legitimised even in the divine plan (divine free will) the supremacy of man over woman, and proposes the establishment of a feminist religion. The author theorises a society of women in which lesbianism is prevalent.

[128] The movement radical lesbians was born in 1970.

[129] There are many female authors who contribute to moderate lesbian theories ('vanilla' or 'rose water' oriented) and extremist lesbian theories ('butch-femme' or 'tomboy-girl' oriented).

[130] A. RICH, *Woman Born: Motherhood as Experience and Institution*, Norton, New York 1976; ID., *Compulsory Heterosexuality and Lesbian Existence*, "Signs", 1980, 5, pp. 631–660.

the series of institutional, cultural and social measures that normatively obligate sexual choice to be oriented to the opposite sex: hetero-sexism becomes the principle target to fight, against, taking precedence over racism, classism, imperialistic colonialism. The author identifies 'lesbian existence' (in recognition of the presence of lesbians and elaboration of its meaning) and 'lesbian continuum' (in lesbian experience as internalisation of female subjectivity), revindicating the female character of lesbians, and lesbianism as internal to feminism. The author investigates what is common to women, what is shared by women, what is different from men in order to develop a political notion of 'sisterhood', placing itself in a critical relation to the theories that emphasise the special qualities of women as they risk sliding into an essentialist conception of 'womanhood' that is inflexible and prescriptive.

On the same lines Germaine Greer[131] speaks of women as castrated or 'eunuch' drawing attention to their condition of inferiority, imposed by males. The author denounces the passive and dissatisfied behaviour of women: the 'female eunuch' is identified with the 'eternal feminine' produced by patriarchy that progressively impoverishes and disables the 'whole woman'. The author adopts the theories of Freudian Marxism, especially those of Herbert Marcuse[132] and of Wilhelm Reich[133] on sexual revolution, believing that sexual liberation and political liberation are jointly implicated, more specifically, that sexual liberation is the premise of political liberation. Greer believes that liberation is possible only through sexual revolution, abolishing the inhibition of libido, the repression imposed on sexual drive, freeing vital energy and human spontaneity.[134] It is in this context that the author thematises gender as cultural construction that has become a sexual 'constraint' for women, their image has been 'castrated' and distorted by two myths, romantic love and marriage based on heterosexual love. A woman's body is the 'battlefield' where women fight for liberation. It is through women's body that oppression works, reifying, sexualising, victimising, devaluing and disabling women. The author believes that revolution is brought about by breaking legitimate social relationships such as marriage and affirming women's self-sufficiency against all forms of dependency, fighting against equality considered "a poor substitute for liberation".

---

[131] G. GREER, *The Female Eunuch*, McGibbon & Kee, London 1970; ID., *The Whole Woman* Alfred a Knopf, Westminster (Maryland) 1999; ID., *The Boy*, Thames & Hudson, London 2003; ID., *Sex and Destiny: the Politics of Human Fertility*, Harper and Row, New York 1984.

[132] H. Marcuse discovers in repressed female sexuality (female eros) the engine of change to overcome the patriarchal social structure. Within the context of the Marxist and Freudian perspective, Marcuse envisages the lines along which to build a non-repressive society that does not subjugate Eros but affirms the pleasure principle instead of the reality principle. Cf. H. MARCUSE, *Eros und Kultur* (1957).

[133] W. REICH, *Die Sexualität im Kulturkampf*, (1963).

[134] In the light of dialectical methodology, the author interprets the following stages: the thesis is formed by spontaneous sexuality, the antithesis of social repression, the synthesis of the negation of negation, therefore the transgression of prohibition, form rebellion to limits.

Chapter 2
From Gender to Queer

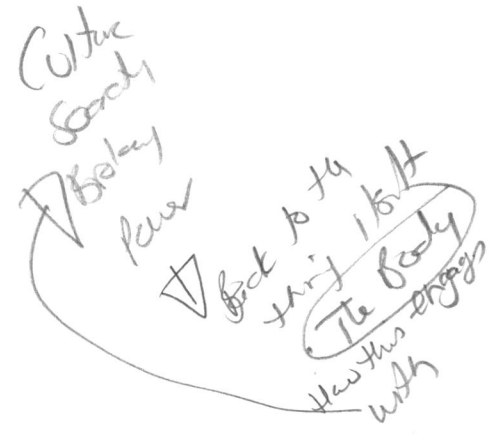

Abstract The theories of gender intersections constitute the first theoretical step towards the postmodern fragmentation of the concept. The gender category undergoes a further profound transformation of meaning in the context of the postmodern deconstructionist perspective. This line of thought radicalises the premises of social constructionism: it interprets the outcome of social construction as a structure produced and organised by power, which should therefore be deconstructed and de-structured ('un-do', according to J. Butler). Gender is considered a fictional construction, without any basis or foundation. According to this perspective, it is therefore necessary to dismantle structures, expose power, cancel each organisation and hierarchy, in order to allow free expression to the multiple, fragmented, contingent individual's will or desire. It is in this context that the category of gender gives way to the queer theory. There are two elements that connote in an innovative way 'queerness' or 'queering': polymorphism and pansexualism, that deny sexual binarism and heterosexism.

Keywords Gender intersections · De-constructionism · Post-structuralism · Pansexualism · Heterosexism · Queer · J. Butler

2.1 Gender Between Modern and Postmodern

2.1.1 A Paradigm Shift in Gender

The reconstruction of the origin and use of the term *gender* across different disciplines (sexual psychology, psychoanalysis, social psychology, sociology, cultural anthropology and feminist philosophy) reveals how, even in the heterogeneity of thematisations, a theoretical common thread emerges: the progressive removal of gender from sex. One may, indeed, speak of a real and increasingly evident separation of the two categories. This separation is justified by a gradual but growing determination to move away from biological determinism and philosophical essentialism, parallel to a progressive estrangement from nature. At first the reference to 'nature' remains in the background, then it becomes irrelevant; finally it tends to be reabsorbed more and more into society and culture.

This separation is introduced with arguments, for different reasons and purposes. Gender is increasingly being characterised as the category of malleability and variability as opposed to the fixity and immobility of sex. Gender is presented as a product of education in psychosexology and psychoanalysis or as social and cultural construction in feminist sociological and philosophical reflection in order to highlight, in a progressively more evident manner, the irrelevance of nature and the significance of the external environment (but also of inner preferences) in sexual identification. The reasons for this trend are attributable on the one hand to the explanation of empirical complexity (in the problematic cases of sexual ambiguity and transsexualism), and on the other to the configuration of different social scenarios for women who claim different roles than those traditionally considered to be discriminatory. The estrangement from nature, therefore, assumes different meanings: that of being the solution to empirical problematicity, but also of liberation from the female condition.

However, until now, apart from occasional brief and marginal signs in the context of psychosexology treatises and in some theories of radical feminism, the existence of nature (although in view of its tendency to irrelevance), and sexual oppositional duality (that is, the existence of two sexes, male or female) are not challenged. Gender is therefore a category we could include in a conceptual horizon described as 'modern'. Modern conceptual horizon is understood as a thought that shares at least one assumption, even in the heterogeneity of elaboration and the different emphasis placed on certain elements: confidence in the ability of reason to develop an explanation of the possibility to know ontological truth, accepted as given and whose existence is not questioned. Dual male or female nature does not constitute a problem, if not only secondarily. With specific reference to emancipationist feminist reflection, both socialist and radical, the modernity of this horizon is further outlined in the acceptance of the knowability of the mechanisms of society and power relations. It identifies patriarchy as the power of the male group over women. There is a negative view of power as domination in the sense of oppression/repression. The self is conceived as having an essence that can/must be freed from the oppression of power, in the optimistic view of the possibility of changing social positions and in the conception of history as progressive and linear.[1]

The paradigm shift in the conceptualisation of gender is evident in the 'postmodern' horizon. A horizon that takes to the extreme what has already partly been developed conceptually in the modern horizon.

---

[1] Cf. C. BEASLEY, *Gender and Sexuality. Critical Theories, Critical Thinkers*, Sage, London 2005, p. 62.

2.1 Gender Between Modern and Postmodern

The reference to the postmodern literally contains the sense of posteriority in relation to the modern, not in a chronological sense: but rather, it indicates a different way of relating to the themes developed in the modern, which is neither in opposition (anti-modern) nor beyond it (ultra-modern). The postmodern conceptual horizon[2] is delineated in different ways, which are traceable in some elements: the lack of confidence in the ability to know a universal or even partial truth, regarding man and society; the denial of the existence and knowability of an order and an essential foundation of human beings (anti-foundationalism and anti-essentialism); the refusal of each foundationalist approach and contempt for a definitive explanation of the real, that unifies the manifold or differences; non-cognitivism as the crisis of reason in the face of acceptance of the complex and contingent shattering of the real. These philosophical premises lead to a chain of conceptual consequences present in postmodern thought: the de-stabilisation of the philosophical structures of Western thought (post-structuralism); deconstruction of the explanations or meta-narratives that claim to know the truth reduced to 'disjointed network' of signs ever-changing and elusive in their dynamicity (de-constructionism); de-centralisation, that is, the peripheralisation of what was believed central and the dehierarchicalisation of what was considered superior/inferior; the fluidisation and liquefaction of the real; the affirmation of power as productive (power, not as 'power-over' but as 'power-to', namely as constitution), in the context of a sceptical vision of history.[3]

It is not possible to make rigid distinctions, which might force the nuances of elaboration. But certainly a paradigm shift can be accepted in the context of thematisation of the gender category between modern and postmodern. In this context, the different theories are nuanced in a continuum that from a strong version moves toward a weak version of the modern, which continues in the weak version of postmodernism reaching its strong or extreme version. As part of this shift there is reference to 'academicisation' of gender reflection intended to clarify basic philosophical problems of concepts such as identity, subjectivity, sexuality, corporeity and the like. Some categories used in the modern are shattered as we move towards the 'disintegration' of the real, but also of the gender category itself.[4]

In this direction there are two thematisations of gender: one directed alongside other categories (gender as 'sexual difference' beside and on the same level as other 'differences' such as race, ethnicity, class); and the other in the direction of the always more explicit connection between gender identity and sexual orientation.

---

[2] On the postmodern concept of gender L. NICHOLSON, *Interpreting* Gender, "Sign", 1994, 20 (1), pp. 79–105.

[3] The philosophers who have shaped the contours of the postmodern horizon are: M. Foucault, G. Deleuze, F. Lyotard, J. Baudrillard, J. Derrida.

[4] J. LORBER, *Using Gender to Undo Gender. A Feminist Degendering Movement*, "Feminist Theory", 2000, 1, 1, pp. 79–95.

2.1.2 The Multiplication of Differences: Intersections of Gender

In the context of recent feminist and postfeminist thought a postmodern orientation is outlined that criticises the centrality of the category of sexual difference in relation to other differences, believing that 'the' difference does not exist but rather that there are 'differences' declined only in the plural. This thematisation involves the decentralisation of the reference to the dimension of sex/gender in the constitution of identity. The sex/gender combination is not discussed in this context (or only marginally) with reference to the nature/culture dichotomy, but instead it is assumed unproblematically, aiming to demonstrate its non-priority, and equivalence in relation to other elements, such as race, ethnicity and class.

The gender category is added to the other categories, introducing an intersection, but also an in-different confusion of elements. The correlation of the categories gender, race, ethnicity, class, intends to highlight the need to put them on an equal position and avoid privileges that produce undue individual and institutional oppression, and therefore inequality. Ethnicity, social status and gender should never be reasons for treating individuals differently: every differentiation is viewed as discrimination. In this sense, the 'differences' cancel out 'the' difference understood as a discriminatory category.[5] The multiplication of differences is intended to divert attention from the centrality of the difference, which is considered the cause of inequality.

In this direction, a postfeminist orientation is REI feminism, acronym for race, ethnicity, imperialism.[6] This is an orientation of thought that contests the feminism related to women and the revindication of their rights: it presupposes white, middle class women, without taking into account the problem of women belonging to ethnic minorities and those in poverty. Often this orientation is referred to as 'post-colonialism', which is a combination of colonialism and postmodernism as an elaboration of a critique not only of patriarchy, but also of the dominant culture, white European and rich, assumed as universal. This orientation is not confined to colonial empires in the factual sense, but in a world of 'global capitalism' it does not distinguish between 'first' and 'third' world, referring to the empire that embraces in a global sense all social, economic, political and cultural inequalities. This approach highlights some elements that traverse gender: racism, ethnocentrism, imperialism.[7]

---

[5] Cf. T. CHANTER, *Gender. Key Concept in Philosophy*, Continuum, London 2006.

[6] Albeit with often disputed terminology (some prefer not to use this term believing that a race in a biological sense does not exist, but only a sociological use of the term), 'race' in this context of analysis refers to black or coloured women living in Western countries, therefore, in the intra-national context; 'ethnicity' refers to women belonging to ethnic minorities, including women that have migrated to Western countries; 'imperialism' indicates women in developing countries who live in Western societies.

[7] B. ASHCROFT (ed.), *Key Concepts in Post-colonial Studies*, Routledge, London-New York 1998; C. MOHANTY, *Feminism without Borders: Decolonializing Theory, Practicing Solidarity*, Duke University Press, Durham NC-London 2003. This is a movement of thought that goes beyond the question of sex/gender, connecting to the theoretical and political movements for civil rights.

2.1 Gender Between Modern and Postmodern

These are elements that affect both men and women, as marginalised and marginal groups.[8]

The rivendications of bell hooks[9] are encompassed in this direction, believing that we can not speak of gender without referring in addition to sexual difference, also to the difference of race and class. Her goal is to expose the sexism, interconnected with racism and classism, revindicating the right to difference, but also to community, non-exclusion and non-oppression. The author believes that the feminist statement 'all women are oppressed' disguises the monopoly and narcissistic privilege of white, middle-class, conservative women, some of which, perhaps, not even had an authentic experience of oppression and suffering. In her view, the hierarchical relationships of power based on race and class are more oppressive than gender hierarchy. In addition, precisely black women who have experienced slavery and racism as well as sexual discrimination, may offer a vision on which to build genuine and articulate feminist politics. The author questions not only the authenticity of the oppression/suffering of white feminism, but also the authenticity of their politics, criticising liberal feminism but also radical feminism that speaks of a common bond among women, considering it insufficient in theoretical and practical terms. In this sense, black women can share with some black men the oppression of race and class, but not of gender. The focus on the issue of race and class tends to dominate if not cancel the issue of gender.[10]

The post-colonial variant of feminism REI is part of the postmodern critique of each homogenising category questioning each and every assumption of a fixed identity, be it of gender, race, ethnicity or class. The criticism is directed against any attempt at universalisation, unification, and standardisation of thought, considered arrogant. On the contrary, this perspective highlights the shattering, particularisation and dynamism. In the context of the critique of European domination of some non-Western countries (in an economic and political sense, but also as regards cultural hegemony) and the binarism that the West opposes to what is 'other', there is criticism introduced to the same category of difference which brings with it the idea that what is different may be inferior. In this sense, it is believed that diversity or otherness ('othering principle') presupposes an oppositional dichotomy between identity or identity groups supposedly fixed and unitary in a hierarchical sense. Difference is perceived negatively, the other/different is

---

[8] It is the birth of 'black or ethnic feminism', in which black women of the Third World are becoming aware of the specificity of their condition of subordination and oppression, not comparable to that of white women in Western societies, criticising racism/ethnocentrism in addition to implicit classism in certain feminisms. Cf. P. COLLINS, *Black Feminist Thought*, Unwin Hyman, Boston MA 1990; I. M. YOUNG, *Justice and the Politics of Difference*, Princeton University Press, Princeton 1990.

[9] BELL HOOKS, *Yearning: Race, Gender and Cultural Politics*, South End Press, Boston (MA) 1990; ID., *Feminist Theory from Margin to Center*, South End Press, Boston MA 1984.

[10] The author is accused of false unification of categories of class and race and of having introduced in the place of gender essentialism a 'race essentialism', presupposing an approved sisterhood of black women, racial unity, giving no room for other forms of racism, apart from black/white racism.

always marginal. This approach plans to deconstruct any difference and dichotomy, with the aim to destabilize the central notion of universal norm and problematise the terms and notions based on identity, recognising and enhancing the plural, fluid and hybrid character of identity.

Gayatri Chakravorty Spivak[11] expresses his criticism of Western thought that develops categories presupposing them as representive in a universal sense, in truth exclusive and exclusionary. It refers explicitly to the deconstructionism of Jacques Derrida, believing that Western thought is based on the recurrence of hierarchically organised dichotomies (man/woman, black/white, good/bad, light/dark), which exclude the other as inferior. Deconstruction is not the reversal of dichotomies overcoming exclusion: the aim is to reveal the mechanisms of their functioning in order to reject them. What is emphasised is the relationship between the dichotomous character of Western thought and the practices of imperialism of gender, rejecting any directive categorisation and pursuing a pluralistic and multiple analysis. There is an emphasis on the hybrid nature of identity, arguing that no strict definition of something is ultimately possible. Each category of identity is provisional and subject to change.

Spivak recognises that the deconstructionist approach, although primarily academic being a theoretical problematisation that fails 'in fact' to give voice to the marginalised, allows an awareness of the privileges and the assumption of ethical responsibility. Deconstruction, eliminating identity and essence, weakens the legal and political practice. The author suggests the notion of 'strategic essentialism', in which the concept of group identity or other homogenising categories can be invoked and used temporarily for pragmatic purposes in a merely nominal and temporary sense, but with a constant perception of limitation and a persistent criticism of their essential status. Essentialism, criticised on a theoretical level, is recovered in terms of pragmatic utility and effectiveness.[12] It is an eclectic perspective that seeks a balance between essentialist/universalist modern thought and deconstructionist/sceptical postmodern thought.[13]

2.1.3 Un-Doing Gender: The Queer Category

The thematisations of gender intersections constitute the first theoretical step towards the postmodern fragmentation of the concept. The gender category undergoes a further profound transformation of meaning in the context of the postmodern deconstructionist perspective.

---

[11] G. SPIVAK, *The Post-Colonial Critic: Interviews, Strategies, Dialogues*, ed. S. Harasym, Routledge, London 1990.

[12] C. SANDOVAL, *US Third World Feminism: the Theory and Method of Oppositional Consciousness in the Postmodern World*, "Genders", 1991, 10, pp. 1–24.

[13] A. MILNER, J. BROWITT, *Contemporary Cultural Theory*, Allen and Unwin, Sydney 2002.

2.1 Gender Between Modern and Postmodern

De-constructionism, closely related to post-structuralism, leads to extreme consequences of anti-essentialism. The term 'deconstruction' is used as a response to Heidegger's invitation related to the destruction of the concepts of metaphysics. It is not easy to give a definition of deconstruction as the authors of this line of thought intentionally evade all attempts to define any concept. It can be said that to deconstruct takes on the meaning of highlighting implicit presuppositions, hidden biases, the contradictions of the categories of traditional thought. Deconstruction has many faces and no hierarchy: it is configured as a methodology for reading the categories of traditional metaphysics, which aims to highlight the gaps, fractures, discontinuities, ideological structures, in place of the alleged unity and uniqueness of intrinsic meaning. To deconstruct means to capture the dissonances and paradoxes that undermine the claim to the all-encompassing and comprehensive dream of systematic theorisation. From deconstruction there has been a linguistic and semantic shift to 'deconstructionism', which classifies, on the basis of the usual patterns of history of philosophy, a thought that in truth is unclassifiable, as the same classification would ultimately limit scope. Deconstructionism denotes the annihilation of the post-metaphysical claim to systematisation and unification. Deconstruction is the revindication of the 'other', understood as that which is unthought of and excluded from any categorisation. It denies the possibility of elaboration of unique and absolute concepts and meanings; it opens to the multiplicity of meanings never fully understandable and formulable as in constant transformation. Every meaning is only a trace of possible absent meanings, a metaphor for something that is not there.

Post-structuralism is closely related to deconstructionism. The prefix 'post', which distinguishes this philosophical current from structuralism, indicates the extermination of the consequences of the concepts as far as dissolving them in the postmodern deconstructionist direction. This thought goes against every structure (perceived as a hidden form of domain), as an organic whole decomposable into elements, whose functional value is determined by the totality of relationships between each separate level and all the others. Post-structuralism intends to de-structure, that is, expose and shake to its foundations every claim to identify structures, in order to exalt disorder and disorganisation, as liberation from the repressions imposed by the structured system.

Post-structuralist deconstructionism marks a radical change in the way of understanding the gender category, bringing it toward the dissolution of the same meaning. This line of thought radicalises the premises of social constructionism. Social constructionism believed that gender was the product of socialisation, namely the construction of meaning in a given society, in a historical era, within a certain culture. Deconstructionism goes further and interprets this outcome of social construction as a structure produced and organised by power, which should therefore be de-constructed and de-structured. Gender as a social construction is a 'compulsory mask' imposed from above, depending on the creation of social hierarchy: it is a fictional construction, without any basis or foundation. There is nothing either in front or behind: indeed, power hides behind. Nature is only presumed, it also being constructed by power just as society. According to this perspective, it is therefore necessary to dismantle structures, expose power, cancel each organisation and hierarchy, in order to allow free expression to the multiple, fragmented, contingent individual.

It is in this context that the social construction of gender is de-constructed, to give space to individual construction. If social constructionism has distanced and separated natural sex to socially and culturally elaborate gender, post-structuralist deconstructionism abandons also socio-cultural gender, moving as far away as to deny natural sex, giving way to 'individual gender'. Just as socio-cultural gender might not coincide with natural sex, now even 'individual gender' could also not coincide with 'social gender'. In short: it is the individual that decides the gender personally desired and wanted, regardless of nature and society. The starting point and the root of gender, in the postmodern perspective, is the individual, not nature nor society. The anti-essentialism, already thematised by social constructionism in relation to nature, is further expressed in relation to society and culture. In this context it is argued that gender 'can', indeed 'should', be regardless of sex. The term gender is used not only as descriptive of a socio-historical process that has occurred/occurs as referred to sex in the past and present, but also and especially as prescriptive, that is, as what must[14] (in the future) on the basis of expression of individual desire.

The postmodern theories of gender refer explicitly to the concept developed by Michel Foucault.[15] Although the author has not directly spoken of gender, his writings have set the stage for postmodern theorising in this category. The author denies the natural sexuality and theorizes sexuality as a result of a complex process of social construction. He speaks of the historicisation but also of the socialisation of sexuality. In his view, sexuality is not a permanent essence of human beings, but it is the product of history, society, context, but also and above all of discourse and power, indeed of 'biopower'. As part of the conception of history as a 'continuum' of repressive practices implemented through institutions created by the power to control society, Foucault traces the genealogy or archeology of sexuality. If before modernity sexuality was governed by religious and moral discourse, modernity introduces it into scientific discourse, in the context of natural sciences as a specific and relatively autonomous sphere.

In the Foucauldian perspective it is biopower that has developed discourses on sex to control the human body and the body of the human species, with birth and population control.[16] According to the author, sexuality is a discursive creation

---

[14] K. BORNSTEIN, *Gender Outlaw: on Men, Women, and the Rest of Us*, Routledge, New York–London 1994, pp. 114–115.

[15] M. FOUCAULT wrote *Historie de la sexualité* in three volumes: *La volonté de savoir* (Gallimard, Paris 1976), *L'usage des plaisirs* (Gallimard, Paris 1984); *Le souci de soi* (Gallimard, Paris 1984). English translation, *The History of Sexuality*, Vintage Books, New York; vol. I, *An Introduction* (1990); vol. II, *The Use of Pleasure* (1990), vol. III, *The Care of the Self* (1988).

[16] Bio-power has developed, according to Foucault, four strategies (techniques and devices of sexuality developed by discourse) of power-knowledge: the hysterisation of the woman's body, the education of the child's body, the socialisation of procreative behaviour, the psychiatrisation of perverse pleasure.

and an artificial invention of power, as an "instrument of domination" or "control mechanism". Each social group is a regulatory structure, which specifically defines bodies, disciplines behaviours in a prescriptive way, excluding other bodies, acts and desires. Identities have the social function of organising bodies and behaviours and controlling, through a reward/punishment mechanism, the bodies and behaviours considered 'normal' and 'natural' in relation to those considered 'abnormal' and 'unnatural', therefore pathological or deviant or even criminal. It is power, through speech, language and society, which gives meaning to bodies, practices and desires.

The French author became the point of reference for the alliance between post-structuralism and feminism. Although Foucault makes few explicit references to women as a specific question or to the issue of gender in his works, his philosophical analysis of the relations between power, body and sexuality has influenced some trends of feminism. Foucault's idea that both body and sexuality are cultural constructs rather than natural phenomena contributed to the feminist and postfeminist critique of essentialism. In this sense gender theories, in the context of post-feminism and postmodernism,[17] become the objects of application of this method. Many theories intend to deconstruct social sex and gender, considering it an important step to liberate the body, identity and subjectivity of the individual from the claim of natural or social essence, presumed as one, simple, homogeneous, static and stable. This perspective breaks down identity into complex, heterogeneous and dynamic identification as a process. With the consequent rejection of all categories: even the same sex and gender categories. Each category has been emptied of content and is used with reluctance, because it always presupposes conceptual systematisation and semanticisation.

It is worth mentioning—even if it is not the object of the present analysis— some critical reactions of certain feminist theories to Foucauldian perspective. There are affinities and tensions between Foucault's theory and contemporary feminism. While there is agreement that Foucault's conception of power contains important insights for feminism, feminists remain divided over the implications of this concept for feminist theory and practice. Some feminists underlined certain limitations in his thought, above all in the political field as regards the promotion of women's autonomy: the tendency of power to reduce agents to "docile bodies" appears problematic, undermining the emancipatory goals of feminism and women's capacity to resist power. Foucault's understanding of the subject as an effect of power threatens the liberation of women, condemning them to perpetual oppression.

The feminist objections to Foucault center around two issues: his view of subjectivity as constructed by power and his failure to outline the norms which inform his critical enterprise, leaving no space for resistance to power.

---

[17] S. AHMED, *Beyond Humanism and Postmodernism: Theorizing a Feminist Practice*, "Hypatia", 1996, 11, 2, pp. 71–93; S. BEST, D. KELLNER, *The Postmodern Turn*, Guilford Press and Routledge, New York–London 1997.

If individuals are the effects of power and 'docile bodies' shaped by it, then it becomes difficult, incoherent or even impossible to explain who resists power. Foucault's normatively neutral description on power limits the value of his work for feminism because it fails in providing the normative resources necessary to criticise structures of domination and to guide programs for social change.

Some other feminists used Foucault's concept of power to develop a more complex analysis of the relations between gender and power which avoids the patriarchal assumption. On the basis of Foucault's understanding of power as 'exercised' rather than 'possessed', as 'circulating' throughout society rather than 'emanating' from the top, and as 'productive/constitutive' rather than 'repressive', feminists have sought to challenge accounts of gender relations from the paradigm of domination/victimisation to a new understanding of the role of power in women's lives, exploring new ways in which women's understand, experience and behave inside the transformation of society. If the feminist liberationist political program aimed to total emancipation of women from power, Foucauldian-influenced feminism concentrates at the micro-political level to determine concrete possibilities for social change, focalising the body as the principal site of power in modern society.

It is in the context of de-constructionism and post-structuralism that the category of gender gives way to the queer theory.[18] 'Queer'[19] means strange, weird, oblique. If it was originally used in a derogatory sense, it is now proudly revindicated by those who were looked down upon with such adjectives. The queer theory in some aspects presents a line of continuity with gender theories, for others it introduces new and even more radical elements that break away from previous thought. The queer theory, albeit partly influenced by certain currents of feminism, does not pose the question of the subordination of women as the object of reflection.[20] There are two elements that connote in an innovative way 'queerness' or 'queering': polymorphism and pansexualism.

Polymorphism is expressed in the radical problematisation and denial of sexual binarism.[21] Queer indicates a way of thinking and living sexuality in contrast to the rigid binary male or female classification. This issue is only marginally found

---

[18] S. Seideman, *Queer Theory/Sociology*, Blackwell, Oxford 1996; A. Jagose, *Queer Theory: an Introduction*, New York University Press, New York 1996; N. Sullivan, *A Critical Introduction to Queer Theory*, New York University Press, New York 2003.

[19] 'Queer studies' is becoming an academic field of interdisciplinary empirical and theoretical study, similar to 'gender studies'. Queer studies also have a narrative and literary value; that differing from the queer theory developed in a philosophical context; many that claim queer is a mere practice. The expression 'queer' was coined by T. De Lauretis at a conference held at the University of California, Santa Cruz, in February 1990 (T. De Lauretis, *Queer Theory: Lesbian and Gay Sexualities. An Introduction*, "Differences: a Journal of Feminist Cultural Studies", 1991, 3, 2, pp. iii–xviii).

[20] R. Carey Kelly, *Queer Studies*, in J. O'Brien (ed.), "Encyclopaedia of Gender and Society", Sage, London 2008, pp. 690-695, esp. p. 693; R.J. Corber, S. Valocchi, *Queer Studies: an Interdisciplinary Reader*, Blackwell, Malden (MA) 2003.

[21] S. Monro, *Transmuting Binaries: the Theoretical Challenge*, "Sociological Research Online", 2006, 12, 1.

2.1 Gender Between Modern and Postmodern

in the reflection on gender of modern thinking. It is, in some respects, anticipated by Money and radical feminism. Queer takes on the value of an explicit rejection of any oppositional binary code.

Queer explicitly expands the gender category to include in addition to the reference to sex also reference to sexuality,[22] as sexual orientation, that is the set of behaviours, attitudes, acts and desires which are aimed at the bond with the other, the attraction towards the other (where attraction is to be understood in an erotic as well as an emotional and romantic sense). The philosophical paths of 'sexuality studies'[23] are outlined in some aspects in a parallel way with respect to gender theories, albeit with certain specificities.[24] Queer goes beyond sexuality studies with the theory of pansexualism, which problematises and denies heterosexuality as privilege in society. There is strong criticism of 'heterosexism', 'heteronormativity', 'heteropatriarchy'.[25] Queer considers each sexual orientation to be equivalent, whether it is expressed towards the opposite sex or the same sex or to both sexes. It is the exaltation of omnisexuality, polysexuality and mulitsexuality, where every sexual preference is justified by the mere fact that it is expressed, at the moment and in the manner that it is expressed.

Queer is therefore an amorphous and speculatively open term: a flexible, fluid, variable, permeable category against closed, rigid, fixed, impermeable dichotomies. Queer represents everything and nothing. The recurrent expressions 'neither/nor' or 'either/or' show the ambivalence and ambiguity that breaks down the oppositional dichotomies of male and female duality. Queer is often referred to as 'umbrella term' which refers to several theories that have a lowest common denominator: the liberalisation of all sexuality in the 'normalisation' of what was considered 'abnormal'.

A widely used acronym is LGBTI indicating lesbian, gay, bisexual, transsexual/transgender/transvestites and intersex. Their common feature is the construction of their gender identities in opposition to biological determinism and essentialism. Their intention is to problematise on the theoretical level and to withstand in terms of practice rigid sexual dimorphism and heterocentrism. It outlines within communities a kind of solidarity among individuals and groups, each different from the other, but joined by the will to provoke the traditional paradigm and transgress and

---

[22] The 'sexuality studies' indicate the critical analysis of the social meanings of sexuality, in reference to the object choice and sexual desire. D. RICHARDSON, *Sexuality and Gender*, cit.; P. SCHWARTZ, V. RUTTER, *The Gender of Sexuality*, Pine Forge Press, Thousand Oaks (CA) 1998. The *'sexuality studies'* place at the centre of the analysis the issue of homosexuality and lesbianism as opposed to heterosexuality, as well as the 'trans' issue that includes transsexuals, transvestites, transgender, and intersex.

[23] Here reference is made to the issue of homosexuality only in relation to the gender debate. Cf. D. ALTMAN, *Homosexual: Oppression and Liberation* (1971), New York University Press, New York 1996.

[24] For the reconstruction of the theoretical paths of 'sexuality studies', see S. JACKSON, *Heterosexuality in Question*, Sage, London 1999, pp. 10-28.

[25] Feminists are, in general, critical of the queer theory, because these theories do not centre on women's issues or even lesbianism.

destabilise the usual social rules, with the intention of dismantling any difference, considered inequality, appealing to equality in the sense of equivalence.

The queer theory rejects any hierarchy and distinction between central/peripheral and primary/marginal both in relation to sexual identity as well as sexual orientation: the difference is considered to be the cause of hierarchy that, in turn, circularly reinforces it widening the distance between normal considered superior and abnormal considered inferior. One can be either a woman in a female body and a man in a male body or a woman in a male body and a man in a female body, both by transforming the body (transsexuals) and also by accepting the ambiguity, hybridity, and male/female coexistence (intersex, transgender). One can be either heterosexual, homosexual, or bisexual.

Intersexuality is exalted as an intermediate sexual condition 'between' and 'beyond' the condition of male and female, as a variant or variation of bipolar sexual determination, as part of a spectrum of continuity with shades and nuances from male to female, and from female to male.[26] The realisation that there are five sexes, in addition to male and female, also hermaphrodites (herms), male hermaphrodite (merms) and female hermaphrodite (ferms), is considered a positive fact that is not necessarily negative or pathological. The non-concordance of hormones, gonads, internal and external reproductive organs, secondary sexual characteristics expands quantitatively and articulates qualitatively the condition and the classification of gender (the so-called 'additional genders'). Masculinity or femininity becomes a 'matter of degree', varying in percentage and intensity from individual to individual, based on the presence or absence of certain characteristics. Queer theory considers it appropriate and indeed a duty to choose to assign the subjects with severe genital ambiguity to a 'third gender', neither male nor female therefore male 'and' female.[27] It is the perspective that believes that each individual should be able to make a personal choice regarding sexual re-assignment or even acceptance of one's own condition, be it even intersex without forced 'normalisation', that is the feminisation of the male or the masculinisation of the female. Hormonal treatments or irreversible surgery on children are therefore

---

[26] A. FAUSTO-STERLING, *Sexing the Body: Gender Politics and the Construction of Sexuality*, Basic, New York 2000; ID., *The Five Sexes: why Male and Female are not Enough*, "The Sciences", 2000, 33, 2, July, pp. 20–25. The author believes that the male/female distinction is a social decision and that the distinction between the sexes is a "cultural need". In this perspective, hermaphrodites that incorporate both sexes challenge traditional beliefs. Cf. also ID., *The Problem with Sex/Gender and Nature/Nurture* in S.J. WILLIAMS, L. BIRKE, G. BENDELOW, *Debating Biology: Sociological Reflections on Health, Medicine and Society*, Routledge, London 2003, pp. 123–144. Cf. also I. MORLAND, *Why Five Sexes are not Enough*, in N. GIFFNEY, M.O' ROURKE (eds.), *The Ashgate Research Companion to Queer Theory*, Ashgate, Farnham 2009, pp. 33–47; J. EPSTEIN, *Either/or—neither/nor: Sexual Ambiguity and the Ideology of Gender*, "Genders", 1990, 7, pp. 99–142.

[27] A. FAUSTO-STERLING, *Myths of Gender: Biological Theories about Women and Men*, BasicBooks, New York 1992.

2.1 Gender Between Modern and Postmodern

deemed illicit, in order that the individual can grow in the intersex state and as adults can choose (or even not choose) on the basis of individual will.[28]

Queer is critical of transsexualism, which forces the transformation of the body's sex according to gender, returning to the conformity of sexual binarism. Queer prefers sexual indetermination to determination. The transgender[29] condition is preferred to transsexualism. Transgender is someone who expresses in the body and behaviour in a transitory or stable manner a gender identity that is disjointed and not aligned to sex. New types are outlined: trans-woman, an individual that is born male and lives as a female; trans-man, an individual that is born female and lives as a male. But also an individual that combines the traits and attitudes of both male and female at the same time or swings from one gender to another with ease. Transgender denotes an individual who 'passes' from one gender to another, with possible and partial modification of the body (surgically and/or hormonally). Transgender also encompasses transvestites, androgens, drag (i.e. those that excessively and outwardly exhibit their sexual ambiguity) and the so-called intentional eunuchus, that is, those who want intentional castration.[30] Some even challenge the prefix 'trans' that indicates and implies a movement from one gender to another, according to polarity to some extent restrictive and limiting.

Queer[31] is any multiple, plural or variable identity; and any behaviour generally and traditionally considered deviant and transgressive. Queer highlights the differences and at the same time the in-difference. It questions stable fixed and compliant identities; it deconstructs individual and social representations; it enhances the indeterminate and indeterminable, in the dynamic search for polymorphic identity. In this perspective, identity does not exist: only identification exists, as a construction always destined to change and to be overcome in everyday experiences. It is the so-called vision of the body as a 'hook' for identity understood as an ever-changing way of life: the body becomes a place where several meanings overlap, continually changing simultaneously and diachronically.

This perspective is also referred to as 'criss-crossing' or 'mixing up' as it enhances the intersection, the mingling and confusion of combinations between self and other. Anatomically female bodies associated with male genders that relate to bodies and genders with the same combination or opposite combinations; anatomically male bodies associated with female genders that relate to bodies and genders with the same or different combination. In the case of transgender, the

---

[28] The author affirms that parents of intersex children are 'brave pioneers' with the difficult task of changing the social perception of the problem, to encourage social acceptance in future generations.

[29] P. Califia, *Sex Changes: the Politics of Transgenderism*, Cleis Press, San Francisco 1997. The term was coined by V. Price. S. Hines, *TransForming Gender. Transgender Practices of Identity Intimacy and Care*, The Policy Press, Bristol 2007.

[30] G. Salamon, *Assuming a Body. Transgender and the Rhetoric of Materiality*, Columbia University Press, New York 2010.

[31] C. Beasley, *Gender and Sexuality*, cit., p. 118.

simultaneous presence of male and female elements confuses the hetero/homo.[32] Confusion and sexual complexity are dominant: according to queer theory, these are also present in some cultures,[33] in the past[34] and in non-human biology.[35]

2.2 Post-gender and Post-queer

2.2.1 J. Butler: Undoing Gender

Judith Butler[36] proposes a theory not easily encompassed within an orientation of thought. She negatively defines herself, as neither feminist nor post-feminist. The systematic reconstruction of her thought is difficult, given the intentional non-linearity of her arguments.

The starting point of her analysis is the rejection of any given, pre-existent and natural element constitutive of an eternal and unchanging essence, at the basis of personal identity. In her opinion there is no absolute truth; no truth in general is knowable in relation to reality, society, power, and in particular with reference to the self. An original, pre-social and pre-cultural male or female sexual identity in this sense does not exist and can not be known: there is no existing starting point of the discourse on sex. The reference to biological-anatomical sex, which seems natural, innate, interior, is produced externally by gender. In this perspective, gender is not derived from sex (according to biological determinism), but on the contrary, gender produces sex.[37]

---

[32] Is a transgender from female to male who relates to a woman heterosexual or homosexual? The answer depends on whether sexuality is considered from the point of view of anatomical sex or social/individual gender. S. PHELAN, *Sexual Strangers: Gays, Lesbians and Dilemmas of Citizenship*, Temple University Press, Philadelphia 2001.

[33] G. HERDT, *Third Sex, Third Gender: Beyond Sexual Dimorphism in Culture and History*, cit.

[34] T. LAQUEUR, *Making Sex: Body and Gender from the Greeks to Freud*, Harvard University Press, Cambridge (MA) 1990.

[35] M.J. HIRD, *Biologically Queer*, in N. GIFFNEY, M.O' ROURKE (eds.), *The Ashgate Research Companion to Queer Theory*, cit., pp. 347–362; ID., *Sex, Gender and Science*, Palgrave MacMillan, Basingstoke 2004; N. GIFFNEY, M.J. HIRD, *Queering the non Human*, Ashgate, Aldershot 2008.

[36] See especially J. BUTLER, *Gender Trouble*, Routledge, New York–London 1990 and ID., *Undoing Gender*, Routledge, New York 2004.

[37] French materialist feminism has examined the sex/gender contrast in this line of thinking, intervening also in the Anglo-Saxon debate. The usual distinction is reversed: it is not gender constructed on sexual biological difference, but sex has become a perceived category, as gender exists. This is the position adopted by C. Delphy, M. Wittig, C. Guillaum, N.C. Mathieu. Cf. C. DELPHY, *Rethinking Sex and Gender*, "Women's Studies International Forum", 1993, 16 (1), pp. 1–9; L. ADKINS, D. LEONARD (eds.), *Sex in Question: French Materialist Feminism*, Taylor and Francis, London 1996.

2.2 Post-gender and Post-queer

In her book on *Gender Trouble*, gender is a socio-historical construction, a "free-floating artifice",[38] the product of the power mechanism by which the notions of feminine and masculine are "naturalised/normalised". Gender does not express the self, an intrinsic way of being, rather it is the effect of a power. According to Butler's view the coherence of the categories of sex, gender and sexuality is culturally constructed through the repetition of stylised acts in time. The repetition of stylised bodily acts establish the appearance of an essential and ontological 'core' gender. The performance of gender, sex, and sexuality locates the construction of the gendered, sexed, desiring subject within what she calls 'regulative discourses'. It is the power that produces gender in society, which imposes the repeated association of social roles to sexual characteristics of bodies. Butler believes that having a male or female role, but also being a man or woman, is the effect of power. Power is not intended as negative oppression, but as constitutive production, as it allows the dynamic, non-uniform, variable formation of gender and sex, as well as their connection. The difficulty we have to separate sex and gender comes from the fact that society constantly and repeatedly accustoms us to associate gender to the corresponding sex.

On Butler's account, it is on the basis of the construction of natural binary sex that binary gender and heterosexuality are constructed as 'natural'. In this sense, Butler claims that a critique of sex as produced by discourse and of the sex/gender distinction is necessary to point out the constructive bases of binary asymmetric gender and compulsory heterosexuality. By showing both terms 'gender' and 'sex' as culturally constructed, Butler offers a critique of both of them. Butler argued that feminism made a mistake in trying to speak about "women" with common characteristics, saying this approach reinforces the binary view of gender relations because it allows for two distinct categories, that is men and women. Butler believes that feminists should not try to define 'women' and she also believes that feminists should focus on providing an account of how power functions and shapes our understandings of 'womanhood'.

The author's aim is to 'un-do' gender, but also sex. The author uses the term 'un-doing', declining the verb 'to do' in the gerund, to indicate the action as a continuous and unfinished process.[39] Un-doing must be understood as de-construction, breaking down, exposing not only natural sexual identity but also the identity of social gender. Sex and gender are both the products of construction: they are fictions that only apparently and outwardly seem real. They must be dismantled in order to realise their non-existence, their artificiality.[40]

In *Bodies That Matter* Butler thematises gender as a 'performative category', being constituted by doing and not being, by the actions associated and associable

---

[38] J. BUTLER, *Gender Trouble*, cit.

[39] 'To make' means to produce, aimed at completion of a final (practical) result; 'to do' indicates an activity or a process without a final outcome.

[40] This is also a thesis of M. WITTIG, *The Straight Mind and other Essays*, Billing and Sons, Worcester 1992. Wittig speaks of nature as an imaginary formation, an idea that "was founded for us".

with sex.[41] She seeks to clear up readings and supposed misreadings of performativity that view the enactment of sex/gender as a daily choice. To do this, Butler emphasises the role of repetition in performativity, making use of Derrida's theory of iterability, a regularised and constrained repetition of norms. This repetition is what enables a subject and constitutes the temporal condition for the subject. In this sense 'performance' is not a singular 'act', but a 'ritualised production', a 'reiterated constraint', under and through the force of prohibition. Iterability is that aspect of performativity that makes the production of the 'natural' sexed/gendered subject possible.

Socially constituted gender creates anatomical sex; it is the former that makes the latter significant in social practice. The performative theory redefines gender as a process or set of discontinuous acts that must be repeated.[42] The sexed body is built from "performed acts", stratified and sedimented. Bodies are passive and receptive instruments of external meanings; they are dynamic facts in a 'growing process'. Butler believes that it is impossible to persist unchanged. Bodies are always becoming; they exceed the norm and reformulate it; they have no limit that confines their development. Bodies, like roles, are constructed by repeated words; they seem natural or social facts, but they are products of regulatory compulsory frames. Men and women, male and female bodies, male or female roles do not exist: there are only 'performances' and 'parodies', repeated and forced by the dominant codes of conduct. One 'is' what one 'does', or rather, what is imposed on the person to 'do'.[43] Butler arrives at immaterialism, the denial of matter itself: matter is not outside language, it does not exist independently before language, but rather after it. But if both sex and gender are constructions of language, the same sex/gender distinction ends up losing importance.

Awareness of the non-natural performativity of sex and of gender is the necessary condition to re-build a gender (as well as a sex) that is individual, not on the basis of alleged intrinsic essence or external expectations of society, but on the basis of desires, drives and the internal impulses of the individual. Gender performativity indicates acting which ends in action-interaction, recognising the variable multiplicity of manifestation of action. The notion of the self that acts (doer)[44] is denied: the self is confined to accomplished acts, it is constructed and at the same time cancelled in the same acts. There is no identity at the basis of the actions, which justifies and motivates them: identity is the product of discursive

---

[41] J. BUTLER, *Bodies that Matter*, Routledge, New York–London 1993.

[42] This theory emerges as original Foucauldian rethinking. Foucault in his 'genealogy' traces the origins of the construction of identity and the subject, but he considers the body a natural given. Butler also believes the (material) body to be socially constructed by performative acts.

[43] A. HUGHES, A. WITZ, *Feminism and the Matter of Bodies: from De Beauvoir to Butler*, "Body and Society", 1997, 3 (1), pp. 47–60.

[44] J. BUTLER, *Gender Trouble*, cit. According to the author, there is no gender identity behind the "expressions of gender".

2.2 Post-gender and Post-queer

acts, the repetition of actions creates the illusion of the existence of the self (gendered core self).[45]

In Butler's view, social gender forces sex into rigid binary categories and behaviours according to predefined patterns and restrictive grids that are always and only male or female. This is a coercive imposition, a kind of 'violence' on the body and actions, suppressing impulses and inhibiting desires which are hindered or prevented of the possibility of expression.[46] In this sense, Butler opposes sexual bipolarity (gender binary) adhering to queer polymorphism, exalting 'gender turbulence', as the plural manifestation of sexual identity (sexless or unsexed, but also multigender).

On these theoretical bases, the author denies natural essentialism and goes far beyond social constructionism. Traditional philosophical categories considered fundamental and foundational are dissolved: the unique, real, rational, universal subject breaks into fragments without a center, sequence, or order. In this postmodern perspective, the subject becomes a point where many confused identities converge, a temporary, nomadic, fluid, unstable crossroads which fractures fixed monolithic substance. The unity and stability of traditional substance are only illusions produced by the iterative performative mechanism.

Butler believes oppositional bipolarity and heterosexuality to be an 'invisible privilege': males/females and heterosexuals are unaware of this advantaged position (just for the mere fact that they belong to a dominant group) compared to the disadvantage of trans-individuals and non-heterosexuals who 'deviate' from the 'normal standard'.[47] In her view, the only possible condition for a 'livable' and publically 'visible' life for the subject, allowing to express the unexpressed and manifest desires and contingent impulses, is to annul what exists in nature before us and which has been constructed socially outside of us. 'Doing' and 'undoing' indicate a circular practise that is never resolved (which recalls the Hegelian dialectic): an "incessant activity in progress", a "productive disintegration" conscious and unconscious; a tool to 'de-naturalise' and 'de-socialise' binarism and heteronormativity. It is the only way to un-learn our natural and social conditions and recognise time and space, to ensure access to the human sphere, free freedom, improvisation of desire expressed in fantasy and imagination, that is always variable, incalculable, unpredictable, by the very fact that it is not rational.

In this context, Butler criticises the Oedipus complex and the incest taboo (that is, the Oedipal-exogamous model), as attempts of psychoanalysis and cultural anthropology to identify a natural structure, that is timeless and meta-social, stable

---

[45] M. LLOYD, *Judith Butler. From Norms to Politics*, Polity Press, Cambridge 2007.

[46] Nomadism (taken up by Deleuze) is a category thematized by R. BRAIDOTTI, *Nomadic Subjects: Embodiment and Sexual Difference in Contemporary Feminist Theory*, Columbia University Press, New York 1994. Nomad indicates the continual mutability of subjectivity; nomadism indicates acentric dislocation, moving 'regardless of the destination'. C.f. also ID., *Patterns of Dissonance*, Blackwell, Oxford 1991.

[47] G. JAGGER, *Judith Butler. Sexual Politics, Social Change and the Power of the Performative*, Routledge, London–New York 2008.

and universal in structuring society and the family as a scheme a priori of normalisation. In line with G. Deleuze and F. Guattari,[48] Butler denounces 'oedipalisation' as a form of colonialism and metaphysical imperialism, critical of structuralism. The author, along the lines of Foucault, believes that the norm as social regulation of all behaviour, proposed as an ideal standard for all (expressed in the Oedipus complex and the incest taboo[49]) is nothing but a form of power that transforms constraint into social mechanism, negative prohibitions into positive controls of normalisation. The norm becomes standard and does not know about the outside (abnormal) or the external (abnormal), incorporating everything. Gender is an index of 'proscribed and prescribed sexual relations', by which a subject is socially regulated and produced.

As part of Butler's radical thought, the only path to sexual emancipation is liberation of the difference, beyond sex and gender, beyond the norm and normalisation. The aim is, through a critical and transformative relationship with nature and society, to make 'visible' marginal identities, living in conditions of insecurity and vulnerability. Freedom is a process never fully realised in the context of the "ontology of fragility". In this perspective, law must not intervene upon the body: every discipline of the body is considered a form of subjugation and submission functional to normalisation. All possibilities of expression and choice upon bodies must be guaranteed, to ensure the proliferation of multiform identities. Norms must be modified in order to expand the spheres of freedom. The goal is to cease to legislate for all, imposing something that is viable only for some and, similarly, to stop prohibiting to all what is intolerable only to few. Social norms should make sexual and gender self-determination possible in every possible changing expression that is never definitive but always susceptible to change.

For this reason, Butler is reluctant to use the concept of identity that tends towards fixing and stabilisation, despite considering it useful and politically inevitable. She proposes 'pastiche' and 'parody', not as a caricature of an original, but as imitation of a mixed identity, that resists fixed and predictable identity. Butler's strategy is transgression as 'non-combinatory art' with unforeseen combinations and mimesis. Her intent is to disrupt consolidated and codified roles, favouring the abnormal, the outcast, the excluded, multiplying queer practices that disturb and re-convert 'vile bodies' into 'bodies that matter'. 'Gender outlaw'[50] is an individual who acts according to gender that does not conform to sex, which does not conform to social expectations, and which is against sexual binarism and

---

[48] G. Deleuze, F. Guattari, *L'anti-Oedipe*, Les Éditions de Munuit, Paris 1972.

[49] C. Lév-Strauss believes that the incest taboo (not as a biological phenomenon but as a cultural one) is the immutable and eternal universal law. In his view, the prohibition of incest constitutes the primary rule of kinship (the prohibition of endogamy and the prescription of exogamy) that defines and codifies family roles in which sexuality is structured, sexed identity and sexual difference (mother/father is someone with whom a son and daughter do not have sexual relations; a mother is someone who only has sexual relations with the father). C. Lévi-Strauss, *Les structures elementaires de la parenté*, Presses Universitaires de France, Paris 1947.

[50] K. Bornstein, *Gender Outlaw: on Men, Women, and the Rest of Us*, cit.

heterocentrism. It is someone who behaves in a different way, provoking customs, beliefs and institutions.[51]

This is the condition, in Butler's opinion, for a 'radical democracy', where the normal and the normative hegemon are no more, somewhere in which to liberate subjective identity, and to put on and dispose of roles.[52] She appeals for the right to not interfere upon bodies, demanding the right to recognize freedom, as expression and recognition of every possible possibility. The only path to give expression to the oppressed, relegated to the 'inhuman' and 'less than human', without recognition. Against the binary order of gender, there must be recognition of every sexual gender, without applying any reference measure by which to judge others. New gender politics is called on to formulate new and plural sexual rights. Butler believes that there should be radical change in the legal and economic institutions to recognise how important the acquisition of gender is to one's own sense of personality, well-being and physical prosperity. Social conditions must be radically changed in order to realise and make possible gender acting.[53]

Butler introduces in this context some applicative proposals.[54]

The author believes that there should not be coercive surgical intervention on children with indeterminate or irregular sexual anatomies. The hormonal and surgical treatment is a form of normalisation of bodies and a coercive assignment of sex. This correction as a regulatory imposition is considered a form of mutilation, a physical and psychological trauma produced by the 'idealisation of the morphology of gender'. If Butler understands the economic reasons of the LGBTI community that want to keep the medical certification of the disorder only in order to have insurance coverage of health expenses (therefore only for instrumental purposes), she stresses that pathologisation may increase stigma. Consideration of this condition as an illness, means to regard it a defect to be corrected, an irregularity to be adapted, leading to internalisation of the sense of social exclusion. The claim to de-patologise intersexuality becomes public recognition of the freedom of sexual transformations as a personal right. In this sense, society must provide the social means to make possible the realisation of the choice of sexual identity, whatever it may be (even in medical and economic terms), accepting the continuity and discontinuity in human morphology.

---

[51] T. CARVER, S.A. CHAMBERS, *Judith Butler's Precarious Politics. Critical Encounters*, Routledge, New York–London 2008; S.A. CHAMBERS, T. CARVER, *Judith Butler and Political Theory. Troubling Politics*, Routledge, New York–London 2008; E. LOIZIDOU, *Judith Butler: Ethics, Law, Politics*, Routledge, London 2007; S. SALIN, *The Judith Butler Reader*, Blackwell, Oxford 2004.

[52] J. BUTLER, *The Psychic Life of Power*, Stanford U.P., Stanford 1997; ID., *Precarious Life. The Powers of Mourning and Violence*, Verso, London 2004; ID., *Giving an Account of Oneself*, Routledge, New York–London 2004; ID., *Subjects of Desire: Hegelian Reflections in Twentieth-Century France*, New York, Columbia 1987; ID., *The End of Sexual Difference*, in E. BRONFEN, M. KAVKA (eds.), *Feminist Consequences: Theory for the New Century. Gender and Culture*, Columbia University Press, New York 2001.

[53] *Ibid*, p. 130.

[54] Cf. M. LLOYD, *Judith Butler. From Norms to Politics*, cit.

In this sense, the author believes that we also need to legitimise transgender status, the moving 'between' genders, as 'interstitial gender', that is transitional and transversal. In this sense, Butler is critical of transsexualism, which presupposes the acceptance of sexual dimorphism. In her opinion the so-called 'gender identity disorders', classified as temporary or persistent discomfort due to a sense of inappropriateness and incongruity between sex and gender, are not psychiatric mental disorders, but merely a 'change' of gender identity.

In this perspective, the author defines sexual orientation as 'the direction of desire', that may or may not depend on gender identity. In her opinion, orientation and disorientation, changes in orientation, not determinable definitively and exclusively are to be expected. The theory of 'transposition' shows that a masculine woman, an effeminate man, a transwoman or a transman desire and may have desires directed to both hetero, homo or bi-sexual[55]. In this context, traditional marriage (relegated to a mere 'symbolic practice') leaves room for kinship as a network of relations that are more or less intense, where not only sexual difference, but also duration, stability, exclusivity, monogamy are not necessary requirements. The rights and obligations of kinship can take countless forms, relations of various natures, regardless of sexual orientation. There is revindication of the legitimacy of any possible alternative form of union. In contrast to the monopoly of the State of forms of recognition, Butler asks for public recognition of any critical and transformative relation to the norms.

2.2.2 T. De Lauretis: Sui Generis

Teresa De Lauretis[56] coined the term queer and proposed a post-gender theory, which in some ways recalls Butler's perspective, although presenting original elements.

Like Butler, the author denies that sex and gender are intrinsic properties or essential inherent qualities of the body, against both biological/social determinism and essentialism.[57] The author believes that sex is not derived from anatomy or biology, but that it is a symbolic construction, or rather a combined effect of many

---

[55] M. SÖNSER BREEN, W.J. BLUMENFELD (eds.), *Butler Matters. Judith Butler's Impact on Feminist and Queer Studies*, Ashgate, Aldershot 2005.

[56] The author is Italian, but has lived in the United States for a long time (she has written both in English and Italian). *Sui generis* has only an Italian edition (Feltrinelli, Milano 1996). T. DE LAURETIS, *Sexual Indifference and Lesbian Representation*, "Theatre Journal", 1988, 40, 2, pp. 155–177; ID., *The Practice of Love: Lesbian Sexuality and Perverse Desire*, Indiana University Press, Bloomington 1994; ID., *The Essence of the Triangle; or, Taking the Risk of the Essentialism Seriously*, "Differences: a Journal of Feminist Cultural Studies", 1988, I, 2, pp. 3–37; ID., *Queer Theory: Lesbian and Gay Sexualities: an Introduction*, "Differences: a Journal of Feminist Cultural Studies", 1991, 3, 2, pp. iii–xviii.

[57] T. DE LAURETIS, *Sui generis*, cit., p. 139.

visual representations and discursive practices, which come from the family, society, and culture.[58] Even gender is a fictitious category, being the product of social normalisation and its 'concrete effects' in social and material life of individuals. In her opinion, sex and gender are representations of the individual's relationship with belonging to a class, group, or category, according to dual structural opposition. The sex/gender system is a symbolic system that correlates sex to cultural contents according to social values and hierarchies,[59] where the cultural translation of sex in gender is characterised by a constitutive asymmetry linked to unequal social organisation.

The new element in the theory of De Lauretis concerns the reference to the 'semiotics of gender' (referring to L. Althusser) and to the process of 'engendering'. In her opinion semiotics is essential to address the issue of gender as a social and subjective construction, it permits understanding of the methods of symbolic construction and transmission of gender, in addition to psychoanalysis, which explains the effects of subjectivation in each individual. The author believes that the sex/gender system is not only a social construction, but also a 'semiotic system', a system of representation that gives meaning to individuals living in society. In this sense, the construction of gender is both the product and the process of its representation. Semiotics constitutes a chain of meanings produced by the process of semiosis. The meanings that through a continuous process of semantic connections and usual associations, produce the subjects and their bodies, in addition to sex/gender correlations. Representations convey meanings which establish roles and positions, in addition to bodies and subjects.

The representations of sex and gender and their connections become concrete reality when they become self-representations, through the subject's own assumption of identity through 'technologies of gender',[60] that is theories and systems that articulate discourse on sexuality. De Lauretis considers the construction of gender as the product and the process both of representation and self-representation.[61] In this way the subject is 'engendered', produced by the assumption and adoption of the categories of the social system. Identification becomes the process of self-attribution of the body for the subject and of the subject for the body, of sex for gender and gender for sex. The author speaks of 'gender self-attribution' and of self-constituted 'engendered subject'.[62] 'Engendering' is the continuous process of attribution of meaning and assimilation that is

---

[58] *Ibid*, p. 139. De Lauretis resumes the reference to *sui generis* parodies, emphasising the concept of 'parody' in ever-changing roles. Each identity is not fixed: it is a parody of another, a simulacrum of something that is not there (nothing is given in its natural fixity).

[59] *Ibid*, p. 136.

[60] T. DE LAURETIS, *Technologies of Gender*, Indiana University Press, Bloomington 1986.

[61] T. DE LAURETIS, *Sui generis*, cit., p. 141.

[62] The author gives a concrete example. When we bar, filling out a form, the box M (male) or F (female) we 'engender': not only do others consider us M or F, but we also represent ourselves as M or F (*ibid*, pp. 144–145).

always reviewable and changeable. It is like a 'wet suit' that sticks to the body.[63] This process produces the body: the body is an abstract social form that is realised when individuals take on a representation of their own. Gender self attribution coincides with sexualisation, identification and subjectification, that is never definite but always indefinite.

The author believes it is necessary to dismantle false ideological representations, dissolving the traditional boundaries of heterosexual and homosexual gender identity (homosexuality itself is considered 'traditional'), to allow the representation of multiple identities, to make 'gender oscillation' visible, the metamorphosis that cross genders regardless of sexes, beyond traditional forms and the hegemonic discourses of sexual organisation. The objective is to build, on a micropolitical level, new figures and new discourses that may 'engender' new and changing identities within sexual (in) difference as well as subjects who in continuous movement transgress assigned boundaries, freeing themselves from gender ideology. They are 'eccentric individuals' who respond and resist the institutional arrangements that they are summoned and subjected by and who at the same time transcend social determinations, who identify and dis-identify themselves, in an always open and never-ending process.

2.2.3 D. Haraway: Cyborgs

Even the queer category is criticised, as it coincides with the same contradictory claim to rigidly define the indefinable. In short, it is unqueer to define queer. Queer is criticised on the transnational level, being a Western Euro-American concept, but above all it is criticised as it presupposes the binarism which it opposes, referring to—in surpassing them—the boundaries of male/female, hetero/homosexual. Queer is criticised because it assumes bodies, subjects and identity.

For this reason the term post-queer[64] is introduced, indicating a new direction, a creative elaboration along the lines of the philosophy of G. Deleuze and F. Guattari (which recall but also transcend Foucault), that radicalises the premises already contained in previous theories. Post-queer is not being but becoming (becoming, expressed in the gerund form to indicate a process), as a permanent state of metamorphosis, transformation, transversal movement. This is made possible only in non-material bodies, that are virtual and bio-virtual, posthuman entities not reducible even to meanings or representations. It is a new sphere outlined by tones laden with imagination, fiction, fantasy, but also irony,

---

[63] *Ibid*, p. 145.

[64] It is proposed not as post-queer that refers to a time after queer, not even as post/queer configuring a going beyond or (post)queer that could favor both 'post' as well as 'queer'. Cf. D.V. RUFFOLO, *Post-Queer Considerations*, in N. GIFFNEY, M.O' ROURKE (eds.), *The Ashgate Research Companion to Queer Theory*, cit., pp. 379–393; D.V. RUFFOLO, *Post-Queer Politics*, Ashgate, Farnham 2009.

2.2 Post-gender and Post-queer

playfulness, provocation and Utopia. Amid science and science fiction, reality and fiction.

Donna Haraway[65] configures, in a postmodern horizon, post-human scenarios of post-queer, introducing the figure of the cyborg. The cyborg is a 'cybernetic organism', a 'hybrid of machine and organism', a creature that belongs as much to social reality as to fiction, but also 'animals and machines together', creatures that populate worlds ambiguously natural and artificial. The cyborg is a technological construction that reshapes the 'docile' body available for manipulation, and transforms it canceling the boundaries between natural/artificial, and human/animal. It is a mixture of forms of life based on carbon and silicon, a mixture of flesh and technology, a biological or bionic body with implants, prostheses and technological systems, but also a humanoid robot with biological parts. It is the reconfiguration of the subject that is deconstructed and reassembled in the transhuman and post-human sense. It is neither machine nor man, neither male nor female. It has neither sex nor gender, is 'asexed' and 'de-sexed'. It does not reproduce, it replicate. In short it is a creature of a post-gender world.

Next to cyborgs appear 'desiring machines' as streams or currents of energy and desire that 'un-do' organisms, breaking them down and reassembling them in a 'rhizomatic' manner, constituting assemblies of various shapes and connections of one point with any other point. They are 'bodies without organs'[66] (BwO) that falsify human anatomy in machinic functioning. Haraway denies the existence of man or nature; she affirms only the existence of a process that produces the one within the other and couples machines.

New technological bodies and dis-assembled virtual bodies that are asexual or perhaps multisexual emerge. It is the definitive cancellation of sex, the overcoming of gender and dualism, the inauguration of a new way of thinking about sexual identity that goes beyond difference. Cyberfeminism becomes a model for a heterodoxy that 'authorises' the ways and forms of subjectivity and desire that escape dominant dualisms in contrast to sexual difference. In this sense, the cyber-entity is a representation for minority and transgressive identities that refuse binarism and hetero-centrism, but also, fundamentally, homo-centrism. The cyborg establishes a new ontology, setting up 'an interactive figure' that evokes new cybernetic modes of relationship, it diffuses and confuses quite deliberately and blatantly dualistic distinctions that underlie our culture, and that between the human/mechanical, male/female, Oedipal/non-Oedipal. It outlines a community as 'fluctuating compilation of subjects' that are historically situated and interact as semiotic and material entities, united by the desire to forge links that do not reproduce the sexist and racist matrix of logocentric thought.

---

[65] D. HARAWAY, *Simians, Cyborgs, and Women: the Reinvention of Nature*, Routledge, New York 1991; ID., *Modest_Witness@Second_Millennium.FemaleMan_Meets_OncoMouse: Feminism and Technoscience*, Routledge, London 1997.

[66] The expression is taken up again by A. Artaud. See E. GROSZ, *Experiental Desire: Rethinking Queer Subjectivity*, in J. COPJEC (ed.), *Supposing the Subject*, Verso, London 1994, pp. 133–157.

Cyborgs, desiring machines and bodies without organs are amorphous entities, acentric, volatile, evanescent. They have neither sex nor gender nor identity. We observe the dissolution of the subject, the destruction of the body, the disintegration of identity that dis-identify, dis-organise and de-territorialise.[67] They disperse and intersect with other fragments of identity. They are only metaphors that we can imagine that represent 'a world without gender', which is perhaps 'a world without genesis', but maybe it's a 'world without end'.

---

[67] A. BALSAMO, *Technologies for the Gendered Body. Reading Cyborg Woman*, Duke University Press, Durham London 1996.

Chapter 3
Gender: From Theory to Law

Abstract Gender came gradually but with increasing visibility into the law, with a considerable spread in the international legal sphere. Initially there is only the explicit reference to 'sex', in the general meaning of sexual identity, as an unjustified reason for discrimination, along with natural, ethnic, socio-economic conditions and political and religious opinions. In this context there emerges a general reference to 'other status' without further specification. The chapter reconstructs the so called 'Gender Agenda', giving a general view of the legal documents referring to 'gender', pointing out the ambiguity of its use and showing the practical implication of the theoretical discussions, with specific reference to intersexuality, transsexualism, transgender, homosexuality. From the Conference of Cairo and Beijing to the Yogyakarta Principles, from the European provisions (sentences and documents) to European legislations, there are widespread and recurrent expressions referring to 'gender identity' and 'sexual orientation', with meanings that go beyond the mere distinction between the biological dimension of sex and the social dimension of gender, to include the instances of postmodern theory.

Keywords Gender identity · Sexual orientation · Human rights · The Yogyakarta principles · Intersexuality · Transsexualism · Transgender · Homosexuality

3.1 Lines of International Declarations and Provisions

The gender category is not only object of abstract theorising. Gender is a reference that came gradually but with increasing visibility into the law, with a considerable spread in the international legal sphere. Initially there is only the explicit reference to 'sex', in the general meaning of sexual identity, as an unjustified reason for discrimination, along with natural, ethnic, socio-economic conditions and political and religious opinions. In this context there emerges a general reference to 'other status' without further specification.[1]

3.1.1 From the Conference of Cairo and Beijing

The introduction of the word 'gender' in substitution of the word 'sex' dates back to the *Conference of Cairo* (1994) and to the *Conference of Beijing* (1995) of the UN.[2] In documents prepared in this context the term 'gender' is often stated in different areas without an explicit semantic clarification and without a clarification of the difference between the biological dimension of sex and the socio-cultural dimension of gender, despite specific requests by certain States suspicious of the ambiguity. The sex/gender debate is introduced in the discussions during the conferences,[3] from which different positions emerge. On the one hand the belief that gender is just a polite substitute for sex, regardless of the semantic background or the moderate perception of the distinction between social roles and biological condition.[4] On the other hand, the awareness of the novelty of this category in the context of the modern and postmodern debate, which is expressed in the attempt by feminist and post-feminist guidelines to introduce it and defend it and the opposite attempt to eliminate it or 'put it in brackets' to highlight the ambiguity.[5]

---

[1] See UN, *The Universal Declaration of Human Rights* (1948): in art. 2 "Everyone is entitled to all the rights and freedoms set forth in this Declaration, without distinction of any kind, such as race, colour, sex, language, religion, political or other opinion, national or social origin, property, birth or other status"; UN, *International Covenant of Civil and Political Rights* (1966): in art. 2.1. "Each State Party to the present Covenant undertakes to respect and to ensure to all individuals within its territory and subject to its jurisdiction the rights recognised in the present Covenant, without distinction of any kind, such as race, colour, sex, language, religion, political or other opinion, national or social origin, property, birth or other status".

[2] D. O' LEARY, *The Gender Agenda. Redefining Equality,* Vital Issue Press, Lafayette (Louisiana) 1997. We may find some expressions as: gender equality, gender discrimination, gender relations, gender disparities, gender issues, gender perspectives, gender methodology, gender approach, gender policies.

[3] Bella Azburg, President of the Woman's Environment and Development Organization (WEDO), maintains that the current attempt to eliminate the word gender and to restore the word sex is 'demeaning' and 'insulting': it is an attempt to turn back the gains made by women, to intimidate and prevent future progress. She doesn't want to go back to the concept of 'biology is destiny', reducing women to the biological dimension.

[4] Selma Ashipala believes that the word should be used with the meaning given in the Platform for Action: "socially constructed roles, understood and expected by the men and women in society, as well as the responsibilities and opportunities for men and women from these roles" (*ibid.*).

[5] Marta Casco, Head of the delegation of Honduras, asked for a precise definition of gender.

The debate shows the lack of agreement regarding the meaning of the concept, as well as the difficulty in translating the term.[6]

Dale O'Leary, in the reconstruction of the debate, stresses that the 'Gender Agenda' sails into communities not as a 'tall ship', but like a 'submarine' determined to reveal as little of itself as possible.[7] The author hypothesises that the lack of transparent use of the category and its 'subtle' insertion might be fruit of a specific well-hidden programme, namely the idea of introducing in law not only a replacement term, but new instances that subvert certain traditional concepts such as maternity and family and the awareness that this disruption might not receive immediate approval.[8]

Subsequently, the gender category tends to assume greater visibility in international documents and has recently acquired a precise and explicit semantic value. There are widespread and recurrent expressions using gender identity and sexual orientation,[9] with meanings that go well beyond the mere distinction between the biological dimension of sex and the social dimension of gender, to include the instances described in postmodern theory.

The Latin American and Caribbean Committee for the Defence of Women's Rights (CLADEM) in a *Declarations of Human Rights from a Gender Perspective* (1998) criticises the formulation of the doctrine of human rights as an historical expression of a western, white, adult, heterosexual male, without any considerations for women, ethnical groups, homosexuals, gay, and proposes the formulation and recognition of the 'right to freedom in sexual orientation and gender identity'.

---

[6] There is consolidation of the use of gender as a non-biological concept (as opposed to sex) but socially constructed, with reference to the influences of culture, the variability in time and the mutability in space of roles, behaviours, personality traits. More recently, the UN and its agencies have adopted a number of definitions of gender that include elements such as social construction and the variability of the concept in history and society, indicating with gender the roles assigned (and the value attributed to them) to women and men in different cultures. As regards the relation between gender and sex, some definitions emphasise the opposition between sex as a static category and gender as a dynamic one. Some of the definitions of the United Nations do not refer to sex or to the biological element, but focus exclusively on the social construction of gender. The United Nations Development Fund for Women, UNDP, the ILO Labour Organization, the Joint United Nations Programme on HIV/AIDS welcome this approach.

[7] D. O' LEARY, *The Gender Agenda. Redefining Equality,* cit. The author demonstrates how 'gender mainstreaming' is a program that the UN asked to incorporate in all commissions, agencies, intergovernmental bodies, consultants, intergovernmental organisations. Cf. G. KUBY, *Die Gender Revolution. Relativismus in Aktion*, Fe-medienverlag GmbH, Kisslegg 2007.

[8] H. PIETILA, *Engendering the Global Agenda. The Story of Women and the United Nations*, Development dossier, NGLS, 2002.

[9] J. JONES, A. GREAR, R.A. FENTON, K. STEVENSON, *Gender, Sexualities and Law*, Routledge, Oxford 2011.

3.1.2 The Yogyakarta Principles

This line is evident in the declaration of a group of experts on human rights known as the Yogyakarta Principles or *Principles on the Application of International Human Rights Law in Relation to Sexual Orientation and Gender Identity: the Yogyakarta Principles* (Geneva, 26 March 2007). The text explains the significance of respect, protection and the realisation of human rights in relation to gender identity and sexual orientation developing and enunciating the reference principles in an articulated manner. These principles intend to draw the attention of institutions and governmental and non-governmental international organisations, but above all to recommend and compel States to direct legislation, jurisprudence and doctrine on the subject.[10] The issue of gender identity and sexual orientation had been treated occasionally and marginally, in a vague and imprecise manner, and sometimes in an inappropriate, if not erroneous manner, confusing the issue of male/female discrimination, with the discrimination of transsexuals, transgender, intersexuals, lesbians, gays and bisexuals. The intent of the document is clarification by the introduction of a systematic and detailed reflection in the sphere of international law both on a theoretical and practical level.[11]

In the introduction to the Yogyakarta Principles the definitions of sexual orientation and gender identity are apprehended. Sexual orientation[12] is defined as <<a person's capacity for profound emotional, affectional and sexual attraction to, (as well as intimate and sexual relations with) individuals of a different gender, of the same gender, or more than one gender>>.[13] Gender identity is <<understood to refer to each person's deeply felt internal and individual experience of gender, which may or may not correspond with the sex assigned at birth, including the personal sense of the body (which may involve, if freely chosen, modification of bodily appearance or function by medical, surgical or other means) and other

---

[10] For a comment on the text cf. M.O'FLAHERTY, J. FISHER, *Sexual Orientation, Gender Identity and International Human Rights Law: Contextualising the Yogyakarta Principles*, "Human Rights Law Review", 2008, 8, 2, pp. 207–248. The *Jurisprudential Annotation to the Yogyakarta Principles* (November 2007) has also been published: it reconstructs the different jurisprudential interpretations of principles in several States.

[11] As introduced by Louise Arbour in *International Conference on Lesbian, Gay, Bisexual, and Transgender Rights*, Montreal, 26 July 2006: *Statement of the Office of the UN High Commissioner for Human Right* (M. O'FLAHERTY, J. FISHER, *Sexual Orientation, Gender Identity and International Human Rights Law: Contextualising the Yogyakarta Principles*, cit., p. 232). This indication has subsequently been developed in the International Commission of Jurists, *Sexual Orientation and Gender Identity in Human Rights Law. References to Jurisprudence and Doctrine of the Inter-American System* (July 2007); International Commission of Jurists, *Sexual Orientation and Gender Identity in Human Rights Law, Jurisprudential, Legislative and Doctrinal References from the Council of Europe and the European Union* (October 2007). The International Service for Human Rights has also contributed to this elaboration.

[12] The expressions 'sexual preferences' and 'sexual minorities' are also used.

[13] *The Yogyakarta Principles*, pp. 7–8.

expressions of gender, including dress, speech and mannerisms>>.[14] These definitions are a reference point in subsequent documents.

The aim of the text is the implementation of regulations to protect these rights and the promotion of a culture which increases the growth of social awareness against transphobia and homophobia, to fight all forms of exclusion, stigmatisation and hatred against individuals on the basis of sexual choice. It indicates in particular: the right not to undergo sex reassignment and to be recognised even in legal documents as intersex or transgender, the right to life, privacy, freedom of thought and public action, economic and social rights (in employment, housing, education, health and safety), the right to a family and to have children, with access to adoption and reproductive technologies. There are many States that have adhered; there are also many critical reactions that highlight the non-binding nature of such statements and recommendations, not being the product of negotiations and agreements. The reasons for non-acceptance of this document are based on the detection of the threat to family, freedom of speech and religious freedom, national sovereignty and democratic institutions, as part of the reference to instances of natural law.[15]

3.1.3 Other Documents

There is also the UN document *Declaration on Sexual Orientation and Gender Identity* (2008). With a reference to a document of the Organization of American States adopted in the same year and which bears the same name,[16] the principle of non-discrimination extended to sexual orientation and gender identity is asserted, the expression of concern at acts of violence against individuals because of their sexual choices, along with a specific request that the Human Rights Council agenda should include discussion of the issue in the hope that Member States will defend these appeals by regulatory action.

The Commissioner for Human Rights prepared a document *Human Rights and Gender Identity* (29 July 2009), highlighting specific issues, offering suggestions and drawing attention to problems in order to inform the authorities and the members of governmental and non-governmental organisations, as well as the public regarding aspects of the debate. In particular, it highlights the fact that gender identity is always treated together with sexual orientation, despite their

---

[14] *Ibid.*, p. 6 and 8.

[15] There have been critical reactions from the Catholic Family and Human Rights Institute, P.A. Tozzi, *Six Problems with the Yogyakarta Principles*, 13 April 2007 (International Organization Research Group, Briefing Paper, number 1, 2 April 2007), Downs, State of America, 9 November 2007.

[16] *UN Declaration on Sexual Orientation and Gender Identity*, 2008.

being separate issues. The document specifically addresses the problems of intersex, transsexual and transgender people, also including transvestites, underlining their right to life, personal integrity and health. It is clarified that the term gender indicates the individual's inner experience that may not match the sex of their body and their own mode of expression (dress, language, behaviour). The document, in the context of EU directives, calls for revision of the gender directives[17] (dedicated to male/female difference) to include specifically gender identity. The study highlights how the condition of transgender individuals in Europe as regards the perspective of human rights is not positive and recalls the Yogyakarta Principles for the implementation of legislation, with particular attention to protection from transphobia, transparent procedures for the change of name and sex in documents, the abolition of compulsory treatment and sterilisation, the accessibility of medical, surgical, hormonal and aesthetic treatment of psychological support within the public sector, the guarantee of the possibility to stay in the family of origin even after the sex change, the sanction of discrimination in employment, the promotion of education for acceptance and tolerance.

The Committee on Economic, Social and Cultural Rights in General Comment no. 20 *Non-Discrimination in Economic, Social and Cultural Rights* (Geneva, 4–22 May 2009, art. 2, paragraph 2) cites discrimination on the grounds of race, sex, language, religion, political opinion, national or social origin, property, birth. It introduces the distinction between sex (referred to physiological characteristics) and gender in the sense of "stereotypes, prejudices and expected roles" that can hinder rights, this reference is explicitly stated in the discrimination of women in pregnancy and maternity in the workplace. In the context of the reference to 'other states' the document refers to the disability, age, nationality, family status, health status, place of residence, socio-economic situation. It explicitly refers to sexual orientation and gender identity, recommending to States that sexual orientation should not be an obstacle to the realisation of rights and that gender identity should be recognised among the 'prohibited grounds of discrimination'.

Lastly, mention should be made to the UN *Convention on the Rights of Persons with Disabilities* (2008). In the context of the fight against historical, economic, social, psychological, and political obstacles, so as to affirm and promote the rights of persons with disabilities, gender is mentioned several times, precisely in the *Preamble* (letter s), in some articles (art. 16, paragraphs 1, 2 and 4, art. 34, paragraph 4 and art. 25, point a), relating to health care and programs that should include the area of sexual and reproductive health. Many documents are critical and expose the 'ambiguities' of the term gender, calling for its replacement with the word sex, explaining that the term gender means sexual difference.

---

[17] Council of Europe, Directive 2004/113/EC and Directive 2006/54/EC.

3.2 Lines of European Regulations

3.2.1 Provisions

Even in community regulations there is increasingly precise, clear and articulate thematisation of the gender issue.

The Council of Europe in the *European Convention on Human Rights* (1950) explicitly recognizes rights and freedoms without distinction as to sex, race, colour, language, religion, political or other opinion, national or social origin, membership of a national minority, property, birth or other status (art. 14) and refers to the right to respect for private and family life (art. 8).

The European Union under the *Treaty of Amsterdam* (1999) and the *Treaty of Lisbon* (2007) explicitly introduces (art. 19, ex art. 13) sexual orientation as a category not to be discriminated along with sex, race or ethnic origin, religion or belief, disability and age. The *Charter of Fundamental Rights* (Nice 2000) in addition to the principle of non-discrimination because of sexual orientation (art. 21), recognises the right to marry and start a family without specifying whether between a man and a woman, leaving open the possibility of recognition of marriage for same-sex couples (art. 9).

Many Resolutions of the European Parliament and the Council of Europe deal indirectly and directly with the principle of equal treatment irrespective of sexual orientation. As part of the general principle of 'gender mainstreaming' along with the question of male/female equality, there is also the question of gender identity and sexual orientation. There are two main lines in the recognition of non-discrimination: the criminalisation of homophobia and transphobia as an irrational hatred of homosexuals and transgender people based on prejudice, like racism, xenophobia, antisemitism and sexism and the recognition of unions also marital, as well as access to reproductive technologies and adoption.

The *Recommendation on Condition of Transsexuals* (No. 1117 of 1989) and the Council of Europe *Resolution on Discrimination against Transsexuals* (No. 1117 of 1989) of the European Parliament explicitly speak of sexual identity, but make no reference to gender identity. The European Parliament in its *Resolution on Equal Rights for Homosexuals* (A3-0028/1994)[18] reiterates that every citizen should have the same treatment regardless of sexual orientation; it calls for the abolition of all laws which criminalise and discriminate against sexual relations between persons of the same sex and the elimination of obstacles to marriage or registered unions of homosexual couples, as well as access to adoption and foster care. In the *Directive Establishing a General Framework for Equal Treatment in Employment and Occupation* (2000/78/EC), the European Parliament and Council of Europe set out the general principle of 'gender mainstreaming' (with reference to the male/female difference) and the prohibition of discrimination on the grounds

---

[18] Preceded by *Resolution on Sexual Discrimination at Work* (1984).

of sexual orientation is repeated, along with discrimination for religious belief, disability and age.[19] This reference is included in the *Directive on the Implementation of the Principle of Equal Opportunities and Equal Treatment of Men and Women in Matters of Employment and Occupation* (2006), which speaks of gender equality, gender mainstreaming and 'integration of the gender dimension', but also of 'gender segregation' as 'sexual discrimination'. The non-discrimination extends to people who have reassigned gender, therefore transsexuals.

The European Parliament resolutions on homophobia (*Resolution on Homophobia in Europe* (2006), *Resolution on the Increase in Racist and Homophobic Violence* (2006), *Resolution on Homophobia in Europe* (2007)[20] introduce the reference to homophobia as an irrational hatred against homosexuals, and also transsexuals (transphobia) based on prejudice; it expresses a firm condemnation of any discrimination based on sexual orientation and gender identity. The European Commission *Proposal for a Directive on the Application of the Principle of Equal Treatment between Persons Irrespective of Religion or Belief, Disability, Age and Sexual Orientation* (2008) explains and reaffirms non-discrimination on the basis of sexual choices.[21] The Committee of Ministers to Member States, *Recommendation on Measures to Combat Discrimination Motivated by Sexual Orientation and Gender Identity* (2010) recommends to adopt legislative measures to implement effectively the fight against discrimination on grounds of sexual orientation and gender identity and ensure respect for human rights to gays, bisexual, transgender, promote tolerance, hoping for appropriate sanctions for discriminatory acts and measures to compensate victims.

Recently, the Parliamentary Assembly with its *Resolution on Discrimination on Grounds of Sexual Orientation and Gender Identity* (n. 1728, 2010) reaffirms the fundamental rights of LGBT people to life, safety, freedom, and recommends to adopt and implement anti-discrimination legislation, and urges to sign and ratify Protocol 12 of the European Convention on Human Rights, which prohibits discrimination in general, provides legal recognition of same-sex couples by recognising the parental responsibilities and interests of children, ensuring identity and security, and calls for the recording in official documents of 'preferred gender identity' with no obligation to undergo sterilisation or medical procedures for surgical and/or hormonal sex reassignment. It reiterates the importance of equality of access to services without bias, ensuring a dialogue between the institutions and the LGBT community. The *Recommendation on Discrimination on Basis of Sexual*

---

[19] In particular, in the premises in paragraphs 11, 12, 23, 26, 29, 31 and in articles. 1, 2 (6), 6. See also Directive 2000/43/EC on racial equality than explicit protection against discrimination for reasons of race and ethnicity in social life (work, education, social security, health care).

[20] For the period 2007–2013 the European Commission, in the PROGRESS programme (Programme for Employment and Social Solidarity) includes gender among the issues of non-discrimination.

[21] The Parliamentary Assembly has adopted several recommendations on homosexuals (1981), on asylum and immigration for gays and lesbians (2000), on the condition of lesbians and gay people in Europe (2003).

Orientation (No. 1915, 2010) proposes to implement the tools of tolerance so as to promote acceptance of non-discrimination.

3.2.2 Sentences and Documents

In the sphere of community jurisprudence, there are many cases reported in international documents on gender issues. Some sentences have gradually recognised certain rights to transsexuals and transgender to insurance coverage for operations for body modification, registration in identity documents, privacy, marriage, social security and some rights of homosexuals, in particular the right to adopt. There are many studies on these issues on a sociological and normative level with the aim of increasing critical awareness of the question, fighting prejudice and discrimination.

The European Court of Human Rights (ECHR) in the period 1986–1998 did not recognise the right to marry to post-operative transsexuals, due to the uncertainty of the nature of transsexualism and because of the differences within various States regarding legal recognition of the new gender,[22] it tolerated the refusal of States to recognize the new gender, acknowledging marriage in the context of the traditional family.[23] It is worth recalling some sentences—without any claim of completeness—that have changed this direction: the case of *Van Kück v. Germany* (12 June 2003) where it is stressed that the medical treatment of transgender people should be covered by insurance; the case of *Christine Goodwin v. The United Kingdom* (11 July 2002) where there is recognition of the possibility of recording sex change in ID documents, claiming the right to gender identity in the sense of conformation of sexuality to individual choice (with or without surgery); the case of *L. v. Lithuania* (11 September 2007) where the privacy rights of transsexuals are recognized, the case *Schlumpf v. Switzerland* (8 January 2009) against the refusal of an insurance company to pay for medical treatment for sex reassignment; the case of *E.B v. France* (22 January 2008) where a single homosexual was not granted the right to adoption because of sexual orientation; recently in the case of *Schalk and Kopf v. Austria* (24 June 2010), the Court held that the refusal of the Austrian authorities of recognition of same-sex marriage does not violate art. 12 of the European Convention on Human Rights, which refers to the heterosexual family: the Court interpreted that provision to be neither an obligation nor a ban on legal recognition of same-sex marriage, rather a permission, believing it possible to recognise homosexual unions as civil unions.

---

[22] *Rees v. The United Kingdom* (17 October 1986); *Cossey v. The United Kingdom* (27 September 1990); *B. v. France* (23 March 1992); *X, Y and Z v. The United Kingdom* (22 April 1997).

[23] *Sheffield and Horsham v. The United Kingdom* (30 July 1998). It should be recalled that the Court held that the prohibition of homosexual relations is a violation of privacy.

The European Court of Justice in the case of *P. v. S. and Cornwall County Council* (30 April 1996), stating that any different treatment with respect to sexual orientation requires particularly serious reasons, seemed to include gay rights in the context of discrimination on the basis of sex (in this sentence transphobic discrimination was considered as a 'sex discrimination' for the purposes of EU law). If in the case of Grant (17 February 1998) it does not believe it should extend the prohibition of discrimination on the basis of sex to discrimination against same-sex couples, in the case of *K.B. v. NHS Pensions Agency* (7 January 2004) it argues that transsexuals should be able to marry and acquire related rights otherwise they would be disadvantaged compared to heterosexual couples. In the case of *Sarah Margaret Richards v. Secretary of State for Work and Pensions* (27 April 2006) it recognises the right to a transsexual to a pension as a woman though born as a man, believing that social security should be extended to transsexuals; in the case of *Tadao Maruko vs. VddB* (1 April 2008) it finds a violation of the principle of non-discrimination by German legislation which does not include the right to survivor's pension in the regulation of same-sex civil unions; in the case of *Jürgen Römer v. City of Hamburg* (10 April 2008) it raises the question of treatment in employment law for same-sex couples, the attorney general calls for equal treatment of homosexual couples and heterosexual couples in the European Union countries, believing that "unequal treatment to the detriment of the people connected to this type of union is a source of discrimination based on sexual orientation".

There have been many studies carried out in this area. The Committee of Ministers of 2 July 2008 decided to take some action against discrimination based on sexual orientation and gender identity. It established an Intergovernmental Expert Group with the task of preparing a recommendation for the 47 Member States of the Council of Europe. On behalf of the European Parliament, the EU Agency for Fundamental Rights has produced a legal and social report on homophobia and discrimination on the grounds of sexual orientation in European Union countries.[24] In this document it is evident that there are no reasons not to extend protection from discrimination to transvestites, to those who live permanently in the opposite sex whether they have undergone medical intervention (transsexuals), either partially or not at all (transgender). This is a wide and articulated sociological and legal analysis (legislative and jurisprudential) compared with an analysis in the context of social discrimination, with reference to employment, freedom of movement, asylum, family reunification, freedom of assembly and speech. The report notes that the sociological analysis is incomplete, given that the stigma is still persistent and the clandestine nature of the phenomenon.

As part of the Parliamentary Assembly, Committee on Legal Affairs and Human Rights, A. Gross has developed a Report on *Discrimination on the Basis of*

---

[24] European Union Agency for Fundamental Rights, *Homophobia and Discrimination on Grounds of Sexual Orientation in the EU Member States*, part I legal and part II social (2008).

Sexual Orientation and Gender Identity (doc. 12185, 23 March 2010) which analyzes the current situation at an international level, aiming to increase critical awareness of the issue, fight prejudice and discrimination, protecting the LGBT community from violence, restriction of freedom of expression and assembly, and to guarantee the right to privacy and family, access to education, employment and health services. In this report the definition of sexual orientation and gender identity explicitly refers to the Yogyakarta principles; it only adds the specific demarcation of sexual orientation in relation to heterosexuality, homosexuality and bisexuality. The text also introduces some definitions: the definition of transgender or trans-people as "people who have a gender identity that differs from the gender assigned at birth and people who want to describe their gender identity in a different way from the gender assigned at birth; it includes people who feel they have to, prefer to or choose to (whether by clothing, accessories, cosmetics, or body modification) present themselves differently from the expectations of the gender role assigned to them at birth". The definition of transsexual as a person who "prefers another gender than their birth gender and feels the need to undergo physical alterations to the body to express this feeling such as hormone treatment and/or surgery". The report stresses the need for explicit recognition of the protection of life, security, personal integrity and dignity of the LGBT community, the legitimacy of the change of name and gender without the need for medical treatment as a precondition, with subsequent recognition of legal status. The document describes the prejudice against homosexuality and argues its unacceptability, estimating that 'alternative forms of family' are on the increase.

3.3 A Look at European Legislations

As regards the laws of the States in Europe, there is extreme heterogeneity. The protection of gender identity is not easy to analyse, as it is an expression that is not explicitly provided for in many laws.[25]

With regard to transgender people who openly declare their gender identity heterogeneous situations are delineated. In some countries (Belgium, Denmark, France, Ireland, Italy, Latvia, Netherlands, Austria, Poland, Slovakia, Finland and the UK) this is considered a form of sex discrimination, without explicit legislation that provides protection as a category, assigning any assessments to the competent bodies or courts, with particular reference to employment and access to goods and services. In other countries (Bulgaria, Cyprus, Czech Republic, Estonia, Greece, Lithuania, Luxembourg, Malta, Portugal, Romania, Slovenia), transgender discrimination is not considered as sex discrimination nor discrimination based on sexual orientation. In few Member States (Germany, Spain) the issue is treated as

---

[25] This reconstruction is based on the general lines of the Report *Discrimination on the Basis of Sexual Orientation and Gender Identity*, 2010.

discrimination based on sexual orientation. In others there exists a specific foundation for discrimination: in Hungary they speak of 'sexual identity', in Sweden of 'transgender identity or expression'.

As regards, specifically, the recognition of the right to change sex and gender reassignment, with recognition of legal status and name change and the ability to marry the opposite sex, there is divergent legislation. Few countries have no regulation.[26] In some countries transsexuals do not have legal recognition (Ireland, Luxembourg, Latvia, Malta). In some countries they are offered recognition if they cancel their marriage, sometimes this is even against the subject's will (especially if they have children).[27] This condition is introduced in countries where same-sex marriage is not allowed. In Europe, the regulations generally impose restrictive conditions (period of observation, medical and psychological assessment, court order)[28] in view of protecting people considered to be in vulnerable circumstances. In Italy and Poland surgical treatment is a requirement.[29] For other countries medical hormonal treatment is necessary and sufficient (Belgium,[30] Germany, Estonia, Holland). Some countries (Ireland, Luxembourg, Latvia and Malta) do not yet legally recognise gender change.

Two paths are emerging. The so-called 'small solution' (foreseen in Germany[31]), where in registry records the change of name is allowed even without the carrying out of surgical treatment; and the so-called 'major solution', where in registry records not only is the change of name allowed but also change of sex, without surgical modification of the body, after having lived consistently with the chosen gender for two years and with medical certification of gender dysphoria.

This is the path followed by English and Spanish legislation. In England the *Gender Recognition Act* (2004) allows correction of birth certificates with reference to name and sex, issued by the Gender Recognition Register. Spain has approved the *Law on the Modification of Sex in Civil Registers* (2007) acknowledging the change of name and sex in registers when these do not match gender identity for the free growth of personality: it is sufficient to be of age, undergo hormone treatment, and have a psychologist's certificate that highlights the incompatibility experienced between biological sex and gender. In March 2009, the Spanish Ministry of Defence repealed the requirement to have male anatomy in order to enter male departments: male or female uniform is not worn on the basis of sex, but on the basis of the identity written on the document.

---

[26] Bulgaria and Latvia.

[27] There is debate about what is the best interest of the child.

[28] In some countries there is no repayment of the national health service, and it is considered a practical deterrent.

[29] Poland has no specific legislation, but recognises the right to legally change sex.

[30] Belgium has issued an *Act on Transsexualism* (2007) with the modification of articles 62bis-62ter in the Civil Code.

[31] In Germany there is a law *Gesetz über die Änderung der Vornamen und die Feststellung der Geschlechtszugehörigkeit in besonderen Fällen* (1980) that allows the change of name and gender in specific cases.

3.3 A Look to European Legislations

No law—to date—explicitly recognises the existence of a neutral gender,[32] it is not possible for a subject (who is intersex or asexual) not to be assigned to either gender or to both. Instead there has been a request to extend the protection granted to transsexuals also to transvestites and transgender.[33] The debate on access to health services remains open. Some think it better for the transgender condition to be classified as a disease or disorder[34] because it guarantees access to medical and healthcare treatment (but not aesthetic treatment or secondary care); others believe that this increases stigma.

With regard to the regulations on homosexuality, it has been decriminalised by all countries in Europe.

In some States there is discussion concerning the possibility of including the aggravating circumstance of homophobic and transphobic acts.[35]

'Hate crimes' are starting to be configured with reference to a physical or verbal attack against an individual, motivated by prejudice against him or her because of sexual orientation. In all Member States currently physical aggression is a crime and in most Member States the punishment for these crimes can be increased if they are motivated by prejudice, for example, against race or religion (in these cases we speak of aggravation). Community legislation does not require Member States to include homophobia or transphobia among the aggravating factors of criminal offenses. Many countries in Europe have provisions for homophobia as discrimination on grounds of sexual orientation (Belgium, Denmark, Germany, Estonia, Spain, France, Lithuania, Netherlands, Portugal, Romania, Sweden, Northern Ireland, Scotland). In some countries even hate speeches against groups are punished: although there is no explicit reference to LGBT their inclusion is intended (Cyprus, Czechoslovakia, Finland, Hungary, Luxembourg, Poland, Slovakia). The regulations in Austria, Bulgaria and Malta are however interpreted broadly. Some countries have hatred on grounds of sexual orientation as an aggravating circumstance of the offense (Belgium, Denmark, Spain, France, Holland, Portugal, Romania, Finland, Sweden, England).

---

[32] This is the direction taken in *Transgendergesetz* (draft law in Germany 2000), which included 'IS' intersex status alongside M (male) and F (female).

[33] S. WHITTLE, L. TURNER, M. AL-ALAMI. (2007) *Engendered Penalties: Transgender and Transsexual People's Experiences of Inequality and Discrimination* (A Research Project and Report commissioned by the Equalities Review) p. 74.

[34] *Diagnostic and Statistical Manual of Mental Disorders* speaks of 'gender identity disorder' as 'mental health disorder'; the International Statistical Classification of Diseases and Related Health Problems of the WHO speak of 'mental and behavioural disorders'. These definitions are widely used in Europe.

[35] In Italy, lively discussion has focused on this area. Proposals have been put forward for a modification of the law on transsexualism in order to recognize the possibility of not changing the body, while living according to the opposite gender to one's sex. There is discussion on the possibility of including the aggravating circumstance for crimes of homophobia and transphobia, and on whether there should be recognition of unions, records or marriage between homosexuals.

As is known, there are many laws that recognise civil unions or marriage, in various forms, between homosexuals. As well as the possibility of adoption and access to assisted procreation.

The countries—among the Member States of the Council of Europe—which have a law recognizing same-sex marriage are: Netherlands (2001), Belgium (2003), Spain (2005), Norway (2009), Sweden (2009), Portugal (2010), Iceland (2010). Other countries have civil unions, also known as registered cohabitation or partnership, which guarantees rights and obligations also to same-sex couples in a way that is substantially equivalent to married couples: Denmark (1989), Germany (2001), Finland (2002), United Kingdom (2005), Switzerland (2007). In France (1999), Slovenia (2005), Andorra (2005), Czech Republic (2006), Hungary (2007) and Luxembourg (2004) granting an inferior status compared to married heterosexual couples. In other countries there is recognition of cohabitation but not a formal record of partnership: Croatia (2003), Ireland (2010), Austria (2010).[36]

Adoption by same-sex couples is legal in the United Kingdom, Spain, Sweden, Belgium, Holland, Iceland. Germany, Norway, Denmark and Finland allow 'stepchild' adoption, which permits to adopt biological (or adopted) children had by a partner from a previous marriage or union. In Ireland and France, both homosexual and heterosexual singles, can make an adoption request. Other countries have chosen to legalise civil unions with unregistered cohabitation, in which certain rights and duties are acquired automatically after a specified period of cohabitation. Unregistered cohabitation is applied, almost exclusively, to heterosexual unmarried couples.

---

[36] There is a lack of recognition in: Albania, Armenia, Azerbaijan, Bosnia and Herzegovina, Bulgaria, Cyprus, Estonia, Georgia, Greece, Italy, Latvia, Lichtenstein, Lithuania, Malta, Moldova, Monaco, Montenegro, Poland, Romania, Russian Federation, San Marino, Serbia, Slovakia, Macedonia, Turkey, Ukraine.

Chapter 4
Identity and Equality in Sexual Difference

Abstract The chapter analyses the arguments and reasons for sexual naturalism, which recognises sex as a natural phenomenon, and for sexual dimorphism, which states that the sexes are two in nature and that they can only be two. The philosophical arguments go through the non-malleability of gender, the constitutive sexual identity and the reasons for complementarity, moving from the de-construction of gender to a possible philosophical and philosophical-juridical re-construction of the relevance of nature in sexual identity and of sexual difference in the family relationship. The goal is to demonstrate the dangers of an in-different or neutral law, the contradictions and ambiguities that arise behind the appeals to equality and non-discrimination as 'equivalence', in order to comprehend and justify the sense of justice (as treating equals equally and the unequal unequally) and the fundamental human rights of the person before the gender claims.

Keywords Sexual identity · Sexual difference · Sexual naturalism · Sexual dimorphism · Complementarity · Family · Equality · Non-discrimination

4.1 Male or Female: The Reasons for Sexual Binarism

4.1.1 A Person is Born Male or Female: The Non-malleability of Gender

The theorisations analysed have progressively distanced gender from sex to the point of a total and definitive separation. Such separation marks the irrelevance of sex and nature, which is placed at the margins and denied in its ontological dimension.

It would be superficial and na today to repropose the theory of biological determinism, the subject of harsh criticism by the gender theories. The theory according to which the biological sex determines the gender from birth in a rigid and unalterable way, presupposing its coincidence, is strongly challenged. The gender theories and recent scientific knowledge teach us 'to take seriously' the complexity of the real. It is not sufficient to refer to the experience of being born as men or women to demonstrate the truth of the sexual binarism assumption.

Even though the classification of the sexual belonging of individuals is generally simple, at times it turns out to be problematic and requires the analysis of various components, not all and not always immediately knowable and understandable. What requires careful consideration is whether the possible complexity of sex determination at birth, but also before or after birth, itself leads to the affirmation of sexual polymorphism. In this sense it is indispensable to investigate the reasons for sexual naturalism, which recognises the sex as a natural phenomenon, and for sexual dimorphism, which states that the sexes are two in nature and that they can only be two.

In order to understand the relevance of nature for the determination of the sex, one has to start from the observation of reality.

Scientific discoveries allow us to observe the different components of sex synchronically: the genetic-chromosomal, gonadic, hormonal, ductal, phenotypic-morphological components. Each component is double and opposite in a female or male sense. The genetic-chromosomal sex is distinguished in 46, XX (female) and 46, XY (male); the gonadic sex, in ovaries (female) and testicles (male); the hormonal sex in androgens (male) and estrogens/progesterone (female); the ductal sex in Muller ducts (female) and Wolf ducts (male); the internal and external genital sex (coinciding with the anatomical sex).

The diachronic observation of the sexual differentiation process highlights 'cascade' modifications coordinated by a non-casual programme, which develops gradually and progressively according to a linear and regular succession of strictly interconnected phenomena. The genetic and chromosomal configuration determines the gonadic morphology that produces the hormones which play a decisive role for the formation of the internal/external reproductive apparatus and the primary/secondary sexual characteristics. This process is organised in a directionality that is not reducible to a cause/effect relationship, but interpretable as a teleological tension towards an end. The anomalies of development are 'dis-orders' presupposing an 'order'; they are irregularities due to factors that interfere with the normal regular process.

The growing complexity of scientific knowledge and the appearance of problem cases—where the different components of the sex do not correspond and develop anomalously owing to various causes—does not mean, on its own, that nature is irrelevant in sex determination and that the plurality of the sexes is better than the male or female opposite duality. On the contrary, they show the intrinsic importance of the nature of sexual binarism.

The theorisation of gender malleability, sustained by Money in relation to cases of sexual ambiguity at birth, has been the subject of criticism on the basis of clinical and scientific evidence. At a clinical level the deep distress of some of the cases has highlighted the problems of sex assignment on the basis of conventional

4.1 Male or Female: The Reasons for Sexual Binarism

and/or merely pragmatic criteria, which do not take into account other parameters coming from nature:[1] feminised males have asked to be re-masculinised. At a scientific level, the discovery of the importance of the prenatal exposure to sexual hormones (to be precise, the cerebral sexualisation in the foetal stage) not only for the hypothalamic imprinting, but also for the psychic identification of the child, show how not only external family, social and cultural psychic factors are determining, but also internal biological factors play a role in the definition of the body image.[2]

Such evidence shows the problematic nature of a sex assignment in cases of sexual ambivalence at birth that is the result of an external decision, based exclusively on the medical criterion of what is easiest—technically speaking—to realise or on the subjective criterion of what is preferred by the parents. The factors present in nature cannot be neglected. They offer important objective indications for the recognition of sex determination, in contrast with arbitrary assignment, which is moreover often the cause of deep traumatic existential problems.

The need arises to understand sexual identity in a complex interaction between natural and cultural, somatic and psychic, internal and external dimensions, univocally reducible neither to the biological factor alone, as maintained by biological determinism, nor to the socio-cultural factor, as claimed by environmental determinism. It cannot be said that everything depends on biology: there are many non-biological elements that interact in the structuring of sexual identity. Nor can it be said that everything depends on society or the environment: biological fact cannot be completely disregarded. Nature is what we are, it is chronologically antecedent and is structurally overriding with respect to society and culture, which constitutively interact with it. In cases of disharmony among the sexual elements, an exclusively physical-biological criterion or an exclusively or prevalently psycho-social one is not sufficient.

These considerations lead us to understand that nature is the critical measure in the establishment of sexual identity. Socialisation is relevant but this relevance is not and cannot be absolute: only within these limits can the nurture theory and social constructionism be accepted. The authentic natural identity 'resists', as not conventionally and arbitrarily alterable by the surrounding environment. Socialisation must be consistent with the biological sex in order to contribute to the completion of the development process. Socialisation is a means and not an end: it cannot alter constitutive biological identity, but rather it can and must accompany it in its development. The cases brought to public attention by Money as evidence of his theory, on the contrary show the non complete manipulability of nature from the outside.

---

[1] J. COLAPINTO, *As Nature Made Him. The Boy Who Was Raised As a Girl*, cit. A critique of Money's theory is expressed by S.J. KESSLER, *Lessons Form the Intersexed*, Rutgers University Press, New Brunswick (NJ) 1998.

[2] M. DIAMOND, H.K. SIGMUNDSON, *Sex Reassignment at Birth*, "Archives of Paediatrics", 1997, 151, pp. 298–304.

4.1.2 Sexual Identity as Constitutive of the Self

Money and Stoller's theorisation of gender malleability (in contrast with the theory of the fixity of sex) posed the premise of social constructionism which, in the sociology and philosophy of feminism, thematised the sex/gender separation in a more and more definite way, considering gender a social and cultural construction, artificial and modifiable. This is the thesis that in turn laid the premises for the extreme theorisation of postmodern deconstructionism with the annulment and dissolution of nature and with it sex, the body, but also of the ego, of the subject. This is the nucleus of the gender theories considered the 'cutting-edge' of the relativist revolution.

From social constructionism to post-structuralist deconstructionism an increasingly marked separation of gender from sex is drawn. Gender feminism grants that nature is the basis of the self and sexual difference, but criticises its constriction in the development of gender. Feminism does not claim the modification of the body and the transformation of the self: it does not want to change sex, it does not reject nature but wants to release woman from the body, perceived as a burden hindering her free expression. The aim is to free the woman of pregnancy, childbearing, childcare which limit her to the domestic-private sphere and stop her from going into public life. Moderate or radical feminist liberation accepts the female body, but asks for a different social role for women or access to reproduction technologies in ways that would allow them to free themselves of constrictions. The problem moves to 'equal' opportunities between man and woman, but this has nothing to do with the body and the natural sex, which are not challenged as such. And yet despite this, at the sociological and cultural anthropological level, social constructionism has theorised the conventional/artificial origin of gender, anticipating, clearly expressing and decreeing the now inevitable scission from sex. In postmodern thought it is this scission that has led to the radical criticism of sex, nature and identity.

This is a new separation which enters into the dualism that periodically returns in the context of western philosophical thought: from Plato (body/soul), through Descartes (res extensa/res cogitans), to the brain/mind theories. The sex/gender separation is the philosophical premise at the basis—even with different reasoning—both of the theorisation of gender malleability (with the consequent prevarication of culture over nature) and of the postmodern theorisation of the construction/deconstruction of gender (with the prevarication of the will over culture and nature). The philosophical arguments which justify the critical nature of this separation and the need to overcome it, offer a thematisation that contrasts on the one hand with the pre-determination of the sex, and on the other with the post-determination and then self-determination of the gender.

It is important to justify the relevance of nature in the establishment of the sexual/sexed identity of the body/subject. It is a question of demonstrating whether philosophical essentialism—postulating the sex/gender coincidence and establishing gender in the sexed body—is still justifiable and in which terms. It is a question of understanding whether gender is a deconstructable construction arbitrarily separated from sex or whether sex and gender are elements connected in the essential identity.

The relevance of philosophical essentialism in the context of sex/gender determinism is shown by means of the contradiction at a theoretical level into which-those denying it-fall. Those who deny philosophical essentialism in the sex/gender determinism deny the substance and substantiality of the body, reducing it to a mere passive receptacle of any desired and wanted form.

Instead, the body is not indeterminate, inert, amorphous or merely quantitative matter. The body is not an impersonal and de-subjectified object, without any 'weight', to be disposed of at pleasure, and which can become anything one wants it to become, susceptible to any transformation or variation desired. The body is not reducible to a 'desiring machine', to a mere assembly of parts and pieces, that can be taken apart and put together again at pleasure. The body presupposes a subject: the very construction and deconstruction postulates the existence of a subject as being a condition of possibility. One cannot 'do' and 'undo' if there is no subject (doer) that does and undoes.

The body is the matter determined by a form; one 'has' the body, but at the same time one 'is' the body. The body is the subject incarnate and presupposes the subject incarnate. If it were only an object or machine there would be no desire or will: desire and will are an expression of the self or subject that 'animates' the body, which makes the body that is and how it is. Desire and will do not exist, but individuals incarnated in bodies that desire and wish do exist. Actions and physical-psychic properties dissolve in performative doing without a subject who guarantees the conditions of unification and permanence of them. The actions are not 'the' subject, but 'of' the subject who acts: they postulate and assume his/her existence.

Sex is not an accidental attribution, but a substantial qualitative determination of the body. Sex qualifies the body in a constitutive and non occasional way. This is also our common experience as well as our reflection: to be sexed is very different from 'hanging a dress on the hanger', as the post-modern liquefaction and fluidisation of gender maintains. Accidental is what can be or cannot be, without the substance being altered: sex however, is a necessary and inevitable determination of the body. Sex is not an irrelevant secondary variable, or anyway on the same level as other variables (like race, class or others) only intersecting with them, but is a constant recurrent element; it is a constitutive element of the human being. Sex, as the basic determination of the body, is also the condition of existing, as well as thinking and expressing oneself. It is the stable and permanent condition that qualifies the subject and his/her identity in time, even in the modification of age, social position or ethnic belonging.

Either the subject's body is sexed or does not exist and it is not even thinkable or expressible. We can not imagine or refer to a neutral individual without a sexed determination. A sexually indeterminate body cannot exist. We cannot even give it a name. Even the provocative and sensational attempts of language do not achieve their goal.

Sex cannot be a matter of mere choice, as our very identity cannot. Indeterminacy is an anomaly that must be determined; indeterminacy as a choice poses itself as a transgression that presupposes determinacy. The polysexual neutral mixing does not exist: we cannot get out from sexual difference, sexual opposition and sexual duality at a cognitive, linguistic, ontological and anthropological level.

4.1.3 The Sexes are Two: Neither Many Nor One Nor None

Having justified the close connection between sex and gender in the substantial determination of personal identity, it is now a question of justifying 'sexual binarism' against 'sexual neutrism', or the necessary opposite duality of the sexes.

The existence of conditions in which it is not easy or immediate to recognise the sexual identity is not in itself evidence of the negation of the opposite duality and the affirmation of the existence of a 'third gender'. In the face of such criticism, it is indispensable to verify the coherence and congruity of the arguments demonstrating that the 'sexes are two', that 'they must be two', that 'it is better that they are two', rather than many, one or none.

'In fact' arguments exist: the psychological distress and the social non-acceptance of sexually ambivalent individuals.[3] The psychological distress is easy to understand, as well as highlighted by clinical studies and psychological and psychoanalytical theorisations; not knowing whether one is male or female undermines the sense and the construction of one's own identity. The difficult introduction into a society built on sexual binarism, rejects and anyway makes the socialisation difficult of those not recognising themselves in the established male and female roles.

The 'factual' arguments, however, are not sufficient: it would always appear possible to demonstrate the opposite. At the psychological level, the reference to ambivalence and original sexual indifferentiation (also outlined by Freud) leads some theories to consider 'sexual neutrality' plausible and even desirable in the name of the fluid dynamicity of the self. Basically, the Oedipus complex and the incest taboo highlight how original desire is not differentiated and not heterosexual. At the social level, the reference to past and present cultures that have accepted and even deified androgens and hermaphrodites opens up to the formulation of new possible scenarios (even though initially difficult if not even tragic) in a future society capable of rebuilding itself accepting sexual multiplicity.

When dealing with these 'in fact' arguments, it is indispensable to analyse the 'on principle' arguments of sexual polymorphism. It is a case of understanding whether sex is only a question 'of degree' or intensity in the shaded variation, or 'of sense'. Why are there only two sexes?

A first answer refers to sexual duality as a condition of the possibility of sociality, understood as a continuation of humanity, of the human kind. In this sense, it must

---

[3] R.W. CONNELL, *Gender*, Polity Press, Cambridge 2002.

4.1 Male or Female: The Reasons for Sexual Binarism

be remembered that the Indo-European root of the word 'gender' derives from 'to generate'. Sexual difference is the necessary and sufficient condition to foster procreative ability, supporting the natural inclination to procreation. Sexual diversity is necessary for reproduction: only simple organisms are able to reproduce without sexual difference by parthenogenesis or asexual reproduction.

One could object however, that the natural ability to procreate can be substituted by technologies that make the reproduction possible by artificial means, splitting nature and procreation.[4]

In fact until today medically assisted reproduction, artificial as it may be, always refers to natural procreation: even with the use of technologies, the embryo is formed by the fusion of two gametes, of female and male origin (whether they come from the couple or from an external donor). Nonetheless, imagining a future world in which human cloning were possible, the conditions would be created for the procreation of an individual from a single individual.[5] The woman could even self-procreate in the man's absence (having somatic cells, womb and ovocyte). If we imagine the possibility of ectogenesis, with the use of the artificial womb and the production of artificial gametes, it could be possible to procreate—and thus guarantee human survival—'without' two sexes. 'One' sex only would be sufficient, but there could also be 'many': it would be the triumph of uni-sexuality and multi-sexuality. Two sexes would no longer be necessary and sufficient.

But, even in this imaginary case, sexual difference would have a sense. Since opposite sexual duality, being a man or a woman, is the condition of the possibility of identity. Identity—the logical one of thought and the ontological one of existence—is possible in difference: an individual is what is (in a positive sense) insofar as distinct/different from what is not (in a negative sense).[6] Identity presupposes difference, as opposition; if everything were undifferentiated, the self could not identify itself, and therefore exist. If there were no sexual difference, there would be no identity. The condition of identity is the recognition of being part and not all, of being a polarity, a point of view that cannot claim to be all, excluding that there exists a way of being, acting, wanting different from self.

Opposite sexual duality is a value insofar as the generator of singularity and heterogeneity.[7] Gender identity is aimed at evading the human search for oneself through the other, through the relationship with the other. The ambivalence/neutrality is a logical contradiction and an unrealisable condition in practice. It is moreover disclaimed by recent medical-biological research showing the man/woman difference (cerebral, hormonal, psychological).[8]

---

[4] This is possible both in a negative sense (not reproducing oneself), by means of contraception, abortion, sterilisation and in a positive sense (reproducing oneself), by means of reproduction technologies.

[5] Clonation by the transfer of the nucleus consists in the transfer of the nucleus of a somatic cell of an individual in a enucleated oosphere. The clone is the genetic copy of an organism.

[6] It is what it is and it is not different from what it is, therefore it is nothing other than itself.

[7] S. AGACINSKI, *Politique des sexes*, Éditions du Seuil, Paris 1998.

[8] See P.J. CAPLAN, J.B. CAPLAN, *Thinking Critically about Research on Sex and Gender*, Pearson, Boston 2009.

In this ontological perspective it is therefore indispensable to abandon the words sex and gender, owing to their vagueness and empirical and theoretical incoherence. It is preferable to substitute them with 'subject/sexed body' and 'gender': 'subject/sexed body' denotes sexual determination as constitutive of the body of the male or female subject and 'gender' refers to the masculinity or femininity as expressions of being and acting insofar as a man or a woman. Sexual identity and gender identity are structured in reciprocal interaction. According to the interactionist perspective between being (nature) and becoming (culture) there is and must be a constant and continuous interchange. The justification for interaction allows the overcoming of the sex-gender separation.

4.1.4 One Becomes a Woman or Man, if She/He Already is

If the sexes are two and must be two, if males and females exist, how is it possible to account for the unit and the difference at the same time?

It is a question of understanding whether it is possible to justify the concept of 'analogy' (denied by the gender theories) in the sense of the relationship of similarity in the diversity between the two sexes as ways of being.[9] It is necessary to verify whether the multiplicity of acts and concepts and the difference between the sexes are analogous (*secundum rationem similem*, according to scholasticism), or instead univocal or equivocal. The analogy is the rational possibility of detecting something common in beings between univocism (taking back of differences to units) and equivocism (affirmation of the differences without units). In short, does a human gender exist beyond the male and female difference?

The gender theories deny the analogy: such negation is the reason but, at the same time, the effect of the negation of the essence of things. In the radical postmodern version, such theories draw inspiration from Deleuze (who draws from Nietzsche's nihilism but also from Duns Scotus, Hume and Heraclitus) and decline the differences in the plural, considering them all equivalent intersections. The affirmation of the equivocity of the being leads to in-differentiated ontology, to the neutral positivity of every difference, in which gradations, variations and oscillations only exist in an immanentist way. The negation of nature arises in the context of nominalism and empiricism, which are at the basis of praxism and historicism, from which originates constructionism, but also relativism and nihilism. Nature is reduced to history and practice. In this perspective the gender theories do not explain how unity and multiplicity can be held together. The theory that justifies identity in difference refers analogously to essence as the permanent structure of sense, transcendent and at the same time immanent: it is the essence that explains the difference between the sexes in the similarity of the human being and justifies the becoming in the sphere of existence.

---

[9] The root of equivocism is the philosophy of indifference and the elimination of the analogy.

4.1 Male or Female: The Reasons for Sexual Binarism

The existential difference of male/female is rooted in the ontological similarity of being human. Men and women are different on existential level, but similar on ontological level (they are both human beings). Humanity is the unitary and permanent substance that justifies the difference of the sexes, besides the qualitative plurality of the characteristics and acts. The human being is the abstract essence, which is sexually declined at a concrete level. Both man and woman are persons, insofar as rational animals or substances with a rational nature.

It is the essence that justifies the coming into existence. The existence of the essence is shown starting from the contradiction into which those denying it fall. The gender theories have progressively extremised the separation between being/becoming in the sphere of the sex/gender separation. Money's theory finds the product of education in gender; social constructionism considers that the gender/sex association can be modified insofar as not bi-univocal and necessary; post-structuralist deconstructionism radically disassociates gender from sex, finding the ultimate root in the changeable drives and instincts. A progressive split between being and becoming can be seen: at first being is denied relevance, then even its existence is denied. One 'becomes' regardless of how one 'is': becoming is arbitrary and subjective, having no objective reference in nature. This is Nietzsche's theory: there is no 'being' behind the 'doing', 'acting', 'becoming'.[10] Gender is a mere artifice created performatively by the will, invented as a conventional category, removed from nature. The motto of the gender and queer theories is 'one becomes the gender s/he wants, desires and feels'. It is only a question of performativity.

But what is the relationship between 'to become' and 'to be'? Is it possible to separate both of them? Is it possible 'to become' without 'being'?

The answer can only be negative. On the contrary: 'one becomes, only if he/she is'. Being is the presupposition and the postulate of becoming. Becoming without being is a chaotic and casual process, which has no beginning and no end, no centre or direction, in which phases cannot be distinguished nor paths be identified. It is the becoming that is lost, that dissolves, disappears, ending up by annulling itself.

In this sense gender/queer is the evanescence of the self, which is reduced to a 'imagined scheme', a crossroads or network which breaks up in the multiplicity of properties and acts. The self is dissolved in the process of do-ing/un-doing that is reproduced indefinitely and never conclusively, always destabilised and destabilising. The becoming, without being, is manifested in a provisional, nomad, fluid, liquid way: a mere confusion and mixing of properties/acts. In this perspective M/F (male/female) are only a 'cluster of concepts' in a spectrum of arbitrarily chosen shades without any clear distinctions. But there would be no properties and acts, the process would not be 'done' if a substantial self did not 'exist', unifying the fragmented and permanent multiplicity, making it possible, perceptible, expressible. The properties/acts presuppose the reference to 'something' or better 'someone' (the

---

[10] F. NIETZSCHE, *Jenseits von Gut und Böse: Zur Genealogie der Moral* (1855–56), English translation *Beyond Good and Evil*, Tribeca Books, New York 2011.

doer) that is more than the sum and the series of the parts, which unifies them in space and lasts in time. Otherwise I cannot say that the properties are 'mine', that the acts are the expression of 'me'. This is why 'becoming' presupposes 'being'.

Even if the gender theorisations refuse the self, annulling the 'being' in the 'becoming', they are obsessed by the self. The 'becoming' is expressed in the proliferation of choices: instead of un-doing identity, it is reborn and is indefinitely reproduced. It can only be like this. But the fluidity of post-gender and queer is in contrast with the real conditions, the actual sexed incarnate individuals. The same queer theorisations realise this when they propose to go back to what is 'human', to the 'self'. It is impossible that they do not recognise at least the stability of the provisional instability that they exalt.

Whoever, against the gender and queer theories, accepts the 'being' and the 'becoming in being', is a 'cis-gender'.[11] A new term, coined in the context of the postmodern theories, which describes whoever lives and accepts the correspondence between their own male or female sexed body and their own subjectivity of man or woman, the concordance between their own sex and gender. Whoever 'cis-gender,' born male and becomes a man or whoever is born female and becomes a woman is a 'cis-gender' (or also gender defender, unqueer, antiqueer). 'Cis' in Latin means 'on the same side' in opposition to 'trans' which means 'beyond' or 'on the other side'. Whoever are aware of how they are born, accepts the way in which they are educated and brought up, behaving and perceiving themselves according to social expectations and structured roles; in short, whoever experiences the coincidence between birth, education, exterior behaviour, interior feeling is 'cis'.

The term 'cis-gender' is extremely provocative. The 'cis-gender' is opposed to trans-gender, taken as a criterion of reference, radically overturning the traditional paradigm: what was normal becomes abnormal. The gender theories that opposed 'normalisation' fall into the same error (and only by inverting it), 'normalising' what is considered 'abnormal'. It makes the very aspirations of the sexual minorities normal. Instead, perhaps, in the name of contingency the infinite varieties should just be left to occur. For a radically sceptical thought, the only way not to contradict itself cannot but be—coherently—that of challenging even itself.

4.1.5 The Variability of the Gender Identity

To affirm that the *sex* is the substantial determination of personal identity and to deny the malleability and arbitrariness of the gender does not mean to go back to the static idea of biological determinism. The existentialist and substantialist standpoint is not static, as the gender theories depict it when they exalt malleability and fluid

---

[11] This neologism was created by Calpernia Addams. It means individuals who have a match between the gender they were assigned at birth, their bodies, and their personal identity. They are also called 'gender normative', or 'cismale', 'cisfemale', and 'cissexual'.

4.1 Male or Female: The Reasons for Sexual Binarism

dynamism. The ontological perspective (the 'becoming in being, or becoming, from being') allows a variability. To allow the variability of gender means that the 'becoming' does not involve predetermined and predeterminable automatisms (otherwise 'being' and 'becoming' would coincide), but it does not even allow approaches of radical arbitrary modification (otherwise 'becoming' would deny 'being'). It is along this intermediate line that a re-semantisation of the gender category is possible, even distancing oneself from the gender and post-gender theories.

Gender is not a construction of society, culture, desire and will, and cannot impose itself arbitrarily on the nature of being. This does not question the fact that the ways of understanding, perceiving and living femininity and masculinity have changed in time and society, and have different expressions in the cultural contexts and can be modified in the future. This does not mean to deny 'becoming', but rather to legitimise 'becoming in being'. 'Becoming' must not be understood as the mere casual and arbitrary movement from one place to another, from one identity to another (trans), but as an Aristotelian 'from something towards something' movement, as a rational recognition in the nature of the sense and the end, of the directionality of development, of the intrinsic potentiality to be actualised. In this sense identity is recognised as the search for harmony between the physical, psychic and social component, as the search for a correspondence between birth, interior perception and social role, in the acceptance of the body's limit and the body as a limit. Gender identity is understood as proving one's sexual identity true, like becoming what one is.

Variability concerns psychological features and social roles (accidental), not the subjects/sexed bodies (substantial). Physical sexual identity is and becomes psycho-social gender, in interaction and integration. Man is and becomes man; woman is and becomes woman by means of the interaction of intrinsic physical factors and external psycho-social ones.[12]

Women tend towards psychological traits and social roles usually marked by childbearing and childcare; men by strength and transformation. Women are more concentrated on taking care (sacrificing the task for the intimate relationship), men on the carrying out of the task (sacrificing the intimate relationship for the task). The changes in the society in which we live however, can lead the woman to be more aggressive or male, without being masculine, or the man female, without being feminine. The masculinity of the woman or the effeminacy of the man can highlight an interference of traits and roles, which must not be confused with the interchangeability of bodies or the confused mixture of identity.

One of the difficult aspects of feminism has been the search for equality in the attempt to include women in an abstract neutral category, cancelling the differences. Female emancipation does not mean negation of sexual identity, femininity,

---

[12] It must be remembered that Butler accuses the Church of 'rebiologising' sexual difference (substituting 'sex' with 'gender'). As can clearly be seen the Catholic Church does not refuse the term 'gender' but the interpretation and constructionist theorisation and takes a critical stance towards biological determinism (*Declaración del término 'género' por la Santa Sede*, Pekin 15 de septiembre de 1995).

maternity; it does not mean devaluation of the body as a prison and disadvantage. Female corporeity can instead be understood as a resource; care as the constitutive element of humanisation.[13] Care can be shared with men, as it is a psycho-social trait and not a physical one. Carol Gilligan herself who formulated this concept in the context of female feminist thought, explicitly recognises that care is a way of acting deriving from women and is more widespread and statistically repeated in the female experience, but this does not deny that men too have or can (or must) experience such a feminine way of doing things.[14]

4.1.6 Transsexualism as the Search for Sex/Gender Harmony

Transsexualism is recognised as a disorder insofar as it expresses a disharmony between the exterior and interior dimension of oneself. This is also referred to as 'gender identity disorder'. The causes leading to such a state (whether organic or non-organic) are not yet clear, but—despite scientific uncertainties—it is considered ethically and juridically important to allow the subject to recover the harmony between the external and internal dimension.

By means of a correct diagnosis it is indispensable for the doctor to ascertain and to exclude the presence of any form of mental disorder, a persistent non-transitory, permanent and irreversible desire, of psychological malaise and interior rift which determine a sense of extraneousness with respect to one's body. The therapeutic surgical-hormonal sex-reassignment strategy foresees a transition period allowing the recovery of a condition of soma/psyche harmony. It is not acceptable that the subject asks for a change as a mere arbitrary choice of will or transitory desire, nor that a doctor goes along with such request without understanding the real motivation behind it, since it would cause harm to the transsexual person.

There must be adequate medical and psychological guidance, hormonal therapy to stop the manifestation of the characteristics of one's own sex and to develop those of the opposite sex. A support is necessary so that a transsexual person may live in the world like a person of the sex to which he/she feels they belong, taking on the gender role that better expresses him/herself. In transsexualism the great trauma that the individual experiences in the transformation of the body by adapting it to the psyche is a sign of the relevance of nature, which cannot be manipulated as one likes. In this sense the juridical recognition of the modification of the body of the transsexual does not coincide with the exaltation of individual autonomy and the devaluation of the body. On the contrary, it introduces an exception to the general principle of the non disposability of the body, so as to

---

[13] C. GILLIGAN, *In a Different Voice: Psychological Theory and Women's Development*, Harvard University Press, Cambridge (MA) 1982.
[14] In this sense the "different voice" does not coincide with the "woman's voice".

guarantee the defence of health, understood not only as a physical dimension but also as a psycho-social one, in both an objective and subjective sense. It also takes on the meaning of a complex search for mediation and integration between the physical and psycho-social dimensions, taking into account the body's signs on the one hand and its interior needs on the other.

4.1.7 The Intersex Condition and Transgender as a Problem

The claim of intersex and transgender persons can be collocated at a different level. Transsexualism expresses sex/gender and therefore body/psyche distress within sexual binarism: this is a question of the femininisation of the male or (more rarely) the masculinisation of the female. Intersexed and transgender persons instead claim the right to form a new status besides the one of male and female: the status of 'neuter gender', which cannot be referred to the traditional states that have always been formulated from the dual opposite sexual viewpoint.

The intersexuals ask to be born and live without undergoing the surgical and hormonal operations of masculinisation or femininisation. They ask to exist as 'neuter' and to be able to choose to remain such, and to be registered at the registry office as IS (intersexual), next to M (male) or F (female).

As can clearly be seen, the condition of intersexuality according to the gender and queer theories corresponds to the condition which in medical literature is called 'disorders of sexual differentiation'. The terminology itself stresses that sexual ambiguities are considered and cannot but be considered pathologies: they are anomalies or abnormal developments not because they diverge from the statistically quantitative prevalence of real phenomena, but because they show qualitatively an irregularity or non-regularity in the masculinisation or femininisation process. A precise early diagnosis is thus indispensable, which carried out during the prenatal phase might make identification possible on the basis of the elements available (genetic, gonadic, hormonal, phenotypic), case by case, of the objective indications (above all detecting the foetal sexualisation at hormonal level) that might lead to a choice of male or female sexual determination that is not arbitrary but suited to the real demands.

Any decision to undergo surgery or hormone treatment, especially if irreversible or difficult to reverse, must be made for therapeutic reasons with the aim of guaranteeing the harmonious well-being of the subject, at a physical-psychic-social level. The operations can never be justified by mere aesthetic reasons, or pragmatic medical choices of technical advantage or by the external expectations of the children's parents. Any medical intervention must be motivated by criteria that will balance the urgency, the gradualness, the predictability of the benefit and the minimisation of damage, where benefits and damage are commensurate to the global well-being of the person, in whom a condition of harmony must be created in the physical, psychic and social components.

After the diagnosis, an early male or female sex assignment is indispensable—as far as possible—promptly intervening surgically owing to medical and psycho-social reasons. This line of action is sustainable on the basis of the following considerations: living with sexual ambiguity involves a psychic trauma, which makes the subjects incapable of acquiring a harmonious sexual identity, and furthermore implies hardship in being accepted by parents and society. On the basis of long-standing psycho-pedagogical experience, the need has been established to waste no time in assigning male or female sex in order to have a clear education right from the start. In this perspective particular attention must be paid to communication, as it is fundamental that the parents and the children themselves are told the truth in the least distressing way, with all the due caution therefore.

In the rare cases in which no decision can be made on the basis of objective evidence, a hasty operation sometimes requested by the parents to calm down their state of anxiety is considered illicit; a vigilant wait is instead licit, a postponement of the operation so as to allow—whenever possible—the active participation of the minor in the sometimes irreversible and traumatic decision to modify their body. In any case a male or female sex assignment is considered indispensable and the consequent education that is able to pay special attention to 'spontaneous inclinations' and to the 'gradual emergence of sexual awareness', of an identity that is different from the one assigned.[15] The choice must be made jointly by the doctor and parents and the correct psychological support for the minor and their parents must be guaranteed, with appropriate counselling, sensitive to their ability to understand through careful and gradual communication.

The proposal of those who consider it legitimate to register a 'neuter gender' in such a situation is unacceptable, since such state would harm and hinder the search for the subject's harmonious sexual identification. Even if there is no evidence of the trauma or the distress that a child could be caused by making him/her grow up physically or psychologically with ambisexuality, the mere doubt that this may hinder a correct existential identification process, causing even serious difficulties in social acceptance, leads to the consideration of the duty to guarantee the possibility of acquiring a sexual determination and an education and consequent socialisation in a male or female sense.[16]

For similar reasons the claim for the legitimisation of the transgender condition is problematic, as the possibility to be and act in the co-presence of male and female elements transitorily or permanently, with partial changes or no change of

---

[15] See Italian National Committee for Bioethics, *Minor's Sexual Differentiation Disorders: Bioethical Aspects*, 25 February 2010 (www.governo.it/bioetica).

[16] The case of adults that have already developed a gender identity that is congruent with the phenotypic sex is different (different from the genetic or gonadic one) and do not manifest a desire for correction: information must be given with care to avoid distress or destabilisations. They must be told the truth however, also to avoid any sort of condition of which one should be ashamed. Particular attention should be paid to counselling and psychological support that is able to balance scientific precision and the emotional state of the subjects, while at the same time respecting the confidential nature of the question.

the body. It is a claim that seems to be motivated also by a desire for transgression: but transgression itself implicitly highlights the reference to nature which is to be transgressed. To transgress means to pass the limits: there would be no transgression if the limits meant to be passed were not implicitly recognised. It is not by chance that the very description of the transgender condition—not always so 'playful' and 'ludic' as presented by the gender theories—unavoidably refers to the male/female opposite difference: to be neither males nor females, or males and females, means to assume the male/female difference. The very affirmation of asexuality or multi-sexuality refers to the original male or female difference which it aims to deny and overcome.

4.2 The Dialectic of the Sexes: The Reasons for Complementarity

4.2.1 Sexual Difference in the Relationship

Sex is not only an empirical fact, that leaves us free to act as we want, on merely individual, drive and instinctual bases. What is important to demonstrate nowadays, in view of the pre-feminist, feminist and post-feminist gender theories, is the normative relevance of sex with reference not only to personal identity but also to the interpersonal relationship. It is a question of explaining why male or female sexual difference takes on importance in human relations. Sexual difference is important in the relationship in the sphere of the interpersonal relationship and in that of the family relationship.

The awareness of sexual diversity—or of the existence of a male or female corporeity, sexually defined in a dual opposite sense—is the condition of possibility for man/woman of the recognition of his/her peculiarity and polarity. The recognition of being a part and not the whole becomes the understanding of the impossibility of an individualistic closure in the claim that only one way of being and acting exists in the world. The structural need of the relationship with otherness is shown, of the coming out of oneself towards the other in order to be able to express oneself completely. Sexual difference is therefore the condition of identity but at the same time of relationship. Human relationality in sexual difference is the condition of possibility of human identity in complementarity.

This theorisation is substantiated by the psychoanalytical theories. In his formulation of the 'Oedipus complex' theory, Freud shows how the psychic structure of identification is sexual bipolarisation; after him, Lacan[17] showed how primary

---

[17] According to Lacan the prohibition of incest symbolically structures the functions and roles in the family: the mother is the person with whom the son and daughter cannot have sexual relations; the father is the person with whom the son and daughter cannot have sexual relations; the mother is the person that can have sexual relations with the father.

sexual difference is the symbolic nucleus (the law of the Father) which controls desire and structures individual psychic life. Also the anthropological-cultural structuralist theories confirm this viewpoint: Lévi-Strauss shows how the taboo of incest represents the constitutive and symbolic modality of the assumption of identity and sexual differentiation, considering family as the possible condition for the acquisition of anthropological identity (the identification of the irreplaceable roles of husband and wife, father and mother, son and daughter, brother and sister) and for the regulation of social structure. At a factual level ethnographical and ethnological studies confirm how the family is a constantly present structure in all cultures.

4.2.2 Heterosexuality as Straight Orientation: The Generation

It is no accident that the word 'heterosexual' has been coined and used in opposition to 'homosexual'. There was a need to define the man/woman relationship after the term had been coined to denote the man/man or woman/woman one. The problem is certainly not one of establishing linguistic precedence as much as understanding the anthropological relevance of such relational modalities. The heterosexual choice is defined by the gender theories with the adjective straight, in contrast to queer. Straight means upright, upstanding, ordinary, linear, without deviations. It is therefore a question of understanding whether heterosexuality is relevant and in what way it takes on a relevance with respect to other types of relationships and unions.

The argument that is used to demonstrate the priority of the heterosexual relationship with respect to the homosexual one is the condition of the natural possibility of 'generation'.[18] The ability to generate (distinguishing human generation from mere animal biological reproduction) anthropologically defines man insofar as man: every man exists insofar as generated, every man exists insofar as generating. In the possibility to generate man discovers and recognises his human relational individuality. In this sense the sexual relationship between a man and a woman makes it possible to procreate naturally (physiologically and genetically). Structurally speaking, this is the missing dimension in the homosexual relationship. Interpersonal affection and the possible duration of the relationship are not being questioned: even if founded on solidarity and stability, the homosexual union is constitutively sterile, and therefore cannot be considered equal to the heterosexual one.

There are generally two arguments opposing the sterility one: the possibility that heterosexual couples can also be sterile and the possibility opened up by reproduction technologies for homosexual couples to have children (lesbians with heterologous assisted fertilisation; homosexuals with heterologous fertilisation and surrogate mothers). The first counter-argument can be answered by saying that

---

[18] 'Gender' derives from the Latin root 'gens', to generate.

4.2 The Dialectic of the Sexes: The Reasons for Complementarity

generative capacity refers to the 'generative potential' of principle regardless of the fact of having or not having children (which could be applied to sterile or infertile couples of different sex and also to fertile couples who do not want to have children). The second counter-argument to a certain extent weakens the appeal to the naturalness of procreation, but not completely in so much as the access to reproduction technologies by homosexuals raises a series of 'additional' ethical issues with respect to natural procreation or assisted procreation for heterosexual couples: the question arises of the legitimacy of the use of technology for subjective desires without therapeutic ends[19] as well as of the problems linked to the use of such technological methods with regard to the unborn child, the donors/donors of the gametes and the surrogate mothers.[20] Moreover, this argument is only valid in the measure in which the technologies are possible and applicable: it is not valid in societies where the reproduction techniques do not exist and would not be valid in a hypothetical future society that experienced a technological regression.

Nevertheless, even if the equivalence between being born naturally and artificially were granted, the child's condition would not be comparable. In the sphere of the homosexual couple, the child would be born into a family situation with two mothers or two fathers, with a 'homo-parenthood', no longer distinct in paternity incarnated in the male body and maternity incarnated in the female one. The child would be structurally either motherless or fatherless, owing to an 'a priori' project. Since the desire for parenthood in homosexual couples is a mimetic desire of the heterosexual couple, with a change in the role of one of the partners who assumes the role of the missing sex, acting 'as if they were' father or mother, even though not having the psychosomatic substance for this, this does not remove the relationship from a structural ambiguity. The danger is that the unborn child is denied the possibility of anthropological and sexual identification with a double sexual referee: the lack of one of the two parent sexual figures involves the risk that the child stays enmeshed in 'parental narcissism' without that progressive separation being established which allows the child to become himself/herself.

The reference to the fact that it is possible, even in unexpected events (such as the death of a parent) or intentional ones (the non-recognition of the child by one parent or the disclaimer of paternity), that a child grows up with only one parent, without their anthropological and social identification being jeopardised, is not convincing. In these cases the child can reconstruct the relationship with the other parent in the memory and the presence of a social family.

The recourse to other forms of socialisation that make identification without mother or father possible is also little convincing and even contradictory. The very fact that it is admitted that the child can (or must) refer to people of the opposite

---

[19] Even though in the case of heterosexual couples, the reproduction technologies do not 'treat' sterility, the reference is used to denote the overcoming of an obstacle or impediment to what could on principle take place naturally.

[20] See L. Palazzani, *Introduction to the Philosophy of Biolaw*, Studium, Roma 2009.

sex of the parents outside the family for their own identification, is proof of the incompleteness or inauthenticity of the homosexual intra-family identification.[21] Moreover, this is an argument that has statistical-factual importance but from which general considerations cannot be drawn. Even if evolutionary psychology were not considered reliable or sufficient and no empirical proof existed of the possible harm to the unborn child owing to the presence of two parents of the same sex, with the very risk that a child's growth in such a family context may trigger off irreparable psychic imbalances, priority must be given to the interest of the unborn child, even sacrificing the desire for homosexual parenthood.

4.2.3 The 'Rainbow Family' as a Problem

The spread of gender and queer theories empties the family of meaning, at least in the so-called 'traditional' sense: it is a term used—in this perspective—only in the plural declination, therefore 'the families'. It is called also the 'ungendered family' or 'rainbow family', denoting the pluri-cromaticity of the multiplicity of choices against the mono-cromaticity of the traditional family. The openness to the alternative or non-traditional forms of family is expressly supported by the LGTBI (acronym for lesbian, gay, bisexual, transsexual/transgender, interssexual) communities. By 'family' is meant—in this perspective—the life together of individuals (single, two, but also more than two) who desire and want to live together (at the moment and up to the moment that they desire and want to) regardless of their gender identity or sexual orientation.

The gender theories consider the broadening of the ways of understanding the family, an historical-social innovation to welcome positively and encourage. The family is considered an accidental phenomenon, variable according to the demands and situations of a liquid and flexible society: it is the individuals and their expression of desire, will and agreement that are pre-eminent. The natural original importance of the family is denied, and it becomes a place of pragmatic sharing or the mere exchange of interests and/or solidarity. What is emphasised is the affective bond of reciprocal support, de-emphasising sexual difference or differences, as well as the duration of the relationship.

At a juridical level in the sphere of the gender theories, the debate returns to the legalisation of civil unions (hetero and homosexual) and the recognition of marriage between homosexuals. The tie of affection which is outside the logic of the law does not come into the debate, as it has an extra-juridical existential and therefore private importance.

The civil union (family not united in marriage or union pacts) foresees the conferring of specific rights and individual and relational duties of a socio-economic

---

[21] X. LACROIX, *La confusion des genres: réponses à certaines demandes homosexuelles sur le mariage et l'adoption,* Bayard, Paris 2005.

4.2 The Dialectic of the Sexes: The Reasons for Complementarity

type. This is a need considered by a consistent line of thought justifiable in the measure in which it is based on the presence of solid affection and tendential stability of both the hetero and homosexual couple, motivated by the intention to build and make plans together. The concerns surrounding the legitimation of homosexual civil unions basically go back to the fear that this might constitute a 'slippery slope' towards the recognition of homosexual marriage, equated to heterosexual marriage and to the possibility of filiation.

Marriage is claimed in the gender and post-gender theories as an individual right of expression of the person's dignity, in their autonomy and in the development of their personality, regardless of gender identity and sexual orientation. Behind the claims for the widening of the recognition of marriage a change can be felt from a philosophical viewpoint, in the very way of understanding such institution, emptying it of its original meaning. Marriage, introduced in law to protect the bond that transcends individual will, limiting its freedom in the identification of duties and reciprocal responsibilities, in the gender theories takes on the meaning of exaltation of freedom in the 'right to get married' (but also in the 'right to have a child'), as the affirmation of the self-determination and free expression of individual personality. Marriage from a natural nucleus based on the public dimension of the promise and the on principle commitment to duration, open to procreation, becomes a merely private and contractual relationship between two adults. There is a contrasting tendency: the institutionalisation of the private union (in the liberalism orientation), and the privatisation of the public union (in the libertarian orientation), reducing the control over the family institution and even de-institutionalising it.

In the gender debate, however, there is far more to this. The 'rainbow families' are not only the civil or matrimonial unions between homosexuals, considered equivalent to heterosexual unions or marriages. Alongside hetero/homosexuality, in an increasingly more evident and explicit way, comes the reference to bisexuality. By bisexuality is meant sexual attraction not limited to just one sex but extended to both sexes, both as attraction deferred in time and simultaneous. In this latter sense bisexuality opens up to a dimension that goes beyond monosexuality, understood as the relationship between two opposite or similar sexes: it does not only place hetero and homosexual relations on the same plane, but widens the relationships beyond duality, granting triadic or quadratic unions etc. In this way monogamy is questioned, generally assumed both in the hetero and homosexual spheres of relationality.[22] Polymory is exalted against sexual monogamism: the co-presence of more than one partner at the same time, creating open ties and consensual multiple relations besides dual exclusiveness, both as polygamy and polyandry.

The queer theories also go beyond the three hetero/homo/bisexuality relational modalities, insofar that they presuppose a sexual bipolarity, in an opposite or

---

[22] J.L. HARITAWORN, C. KLESSE, *Poly/logue: a Critical Introduction to Polyamory*, "Sexualities", 2006, 9 (5), pp. 515–529.

homologous way, confirming or denying sexual difference. Not only heteronormativity, but also homo/binormativity are beginning to be feared, as they are perceived as limiting with respect to the 'rainbow' of sexual differences which exalts unstable and changeable indeterminateness in sexual relations, made up also of relations between transgender and intersex persons or with males and/or females. There is the exaltation of any preference or sexual tendency therefore granting (implicitly but at times also explicitly) also incest, paedophilia, zoophilia, or any other kind of sexual choice.[23] Starting from the freedom of choice with respect to identity and sexual orientation, family ties are irrespective not only of the sexual belonging of the partner but also of the number of partners, parental ties, age or whatever else. It is here that the inevitable 'slippery slope' appears, intentionally or unconsciously, connected to the gender and post-gender theorisations. Every sexual choice (individual and relational) becomes equivalent to any other, indifferently. This is intuitively as well as philosophically unacceptable: the reason for which equivalence with respect to non-equivalence must be privileged is not justified in reference to different conditions.

The task of the philosophy of law is 'demythologisation', to 'expose' the myths of the law, often 'not innocent', insofar as used to give society an image of itself that does not correspond to its real structure. And in the sphere of the juridical debate on the family the contrasting myths are to be seen in the alternation and contrast between 'institutional' myth and 'evolutionist' myth, one founded on the structural provisions safeguarding the family such as community, the other on the changeability and dynamicity of the norms protecting the claims of individuals. In today's liberalist and liberationist society, there is a tendency to valorise the second myth with respect to the first, considered traditional, conservative and now outdated: individualism and contingency claim to oust relationality and persistence. The task of the philosophy of law is to show that the family persists even in the 'mutations', since the myth of monadic unrelated individualism does not correspond to the meaning of the law. It is the conscience of the relationship, as the basis of identity, which marks the way towards the demythologisation of individualism and the reconfirmation of the anthropological dialogic-communicative paradigm, through the reconfirmation of the real meaning of the law in the family. The jurists are called upon to bring their specific contribution, highlighting how the objective structure of the family must be taken seriously. The family is not the conventional product of a society and a culture, nor even less so the fruit of contingent individual choices: the family is a reality that existed before the law, and the law cannot but recognise and protect it in its anthropological and structural significance.

---

[23] See J. Butler and the queer theories.

4.3 Gender Between Equality and Non Discrimination

4.3.1 The Ambiguities of Equality: Treating Equals Equally and the Unequal Unequally

With reference to both gender identity and sexual orientation the gender and queer claims have a common element: the appeal to equality and non discrimination.

But what is meant exactly by equality? It is important to start off with a general definition of the concept. Equality denotes the substitutability between two terms in the same context. Equality does not coincide with identity, but presupposes diversity: only if two things are different (even though having relevant similar characteristics) can they be equal, otherwise they would be identical. For the same reason inequality does not coincide with difference, even assuming it: the reference to inequality denotes that when compared, things do not have relevant similar characteristics. The condition therefore to semantically define equality and inequality is the individuation and justification of the relevant or irrelevant similarity between the different terms being compared.

Juridically speaking, the principle of equality concerns treatment with respect to individuals or groups of individuals. The problem is to understand who is equal and unequal on the basis of the similarity or non similarity in the relevant characteristics, but above all why a person is equal or unequal, in order to consequently understand how and why they are treated in a certain way.

It must be stressed that to treat equally does not mean to treat everyone in the same way. This would involve the non consideration of the differences and therefore 'in-difference', which would be expressed in the annulment or cancellation of the differences or in the homologation, standardisation or assimilation of the differences. In this way equality would become the discrimination of diversity.

This is a complex study that progressively appeared in the sphere of feminist thought. A number of feminist theories criticise the principle of equality, claimed in the first wave of feminism, in so much as an abstract principle that neutralises the differences, even differences between the sexes, ending up by introducing the discrimination of sexual diversity. The women who at the beginning fought to be equal to men, realised that equality hid the discrimination of their difference: women are different from men, and so if they are treated 'like' men they are unduly assimilated into them and discriminated against. In this sense the awareness arises that the recognition of equal dignity and equal opportunities to individuals involves the introduction of similar but also different treatment, by reason of the similarity and relevant diversity.

In the gender theories between modern and post-modern the way of understanding equality is radically modified. Equality is claimed, holding that the different treatment of transsexuals, intersex and transgender persons, homosexuals and bisexuals with respect to heterosexual males and females, is discriminating and discriminatory. An indifferent equality of sexual orientations is claimed with respect to different or similar sex, demanding the equalisation of the rights in each context, in the free expression of thought, social participation, but also in the family sphere. There is just one exception: the claim of the introduction of an aggravating circumstance for the punishment of offences of transphobia and homophobia which presupposes and foresees different treatment.

4.3.2 Women and Men: Equal and Different Before the Law

In the context of feminism, reflections have always placed the equality/difference opposition at the centre of attention. But the equality/difference pairing is an incorrect opposition at a semantic as well as philosophical level.[24] The ambiguity of a certain part of feminism arises from the confusion between equality and identity: some feminists have realised that equality does not mean identity (women are equal, but not identical to men), but it means recognition of diversity, and the distinction of a consequent different treatment. It is a question of understanding whether the claim to consider the man/woman sexual difference is compatible or incompatible with the principle of equality.

To treat equally means to recognise every human being equal dignity, in an abstract and universal dimension which is referred to 'everyone'. Equality is opposed to and must oppose arbitrary privileges and discrimination on the basis of exterior features, ethnic group, social or economic standing, political or religious beliefs, chronological, existential or physical-psychic conditions (for example, of ability and disability).

Equality precedes diversity in the law. The centrifugal-diffusive dynamism that constitutively characterises the law places the emphasis on the universal logic that encompasses diversity. The law considers the human being in as much as a human being, in his dimension common to all human beings (the possession of reason), in the ontological and relational dimension, regardless of the differentiations. In this sense, the law cannot renounce the principle of equality, except at the cost of denying its original vocation. One can say that the recognition of equality is the condition of the very possibility of the law: equality is the 'quantifier of universalisation' which makes it possible to extend the recognition of rights to all human beings, regardless of their differences, even sexual ones.

But this is true in a structural sense: the law cannot and must not absolutise equality understood as a fact at an existential level, even though recognising it as a supreme value. The absolutisation of equality would have the ignorance and flattening of diversity as its consequence. In this sense the ontological meaning of the law must be integrated with the reference to the regulating value of justice, which provides for 'giving to every man his own', avoiding treating the unequal

---

[24] Equality is a relationship between two entities (subjects or objects) in the measure in which they possess the same relevant characteristic (or if they possess in the same measure the relevant characteristic) in the context or universe of discourse in which the judgement of equality is.

equally and with particular reference to equity, or justice of the single case, which makes it possible to resolve the aporias of equality, progressively adjusting the law to concrete diversity.[25] In other words, the ontologically universal law 'of principle', cannot neglect existential diversity 'of fact', but instead must make an effort to consider it in a fair unbiased way.

This does not mean that equality gives way to diversity: equality must remain the ultimate foundation of the law, even in the just and equitable consideration of existential diversity. The absence of a hierarchy between equity and diversity (where the former is superior to the latter), of a balance between law, justice and equity, can lead to two outcomes, both dangerous: undifferentiated equality and unequal difference. The first results in homogenisation, or treating the unequal equally: the second in the unilateral imposition of a difference, unjustly assumed to be superior with respect to others neglecting the common elements, therefore treating the equal unequally. It is possible to avoid such dangers by distinguishing the ontological level from the ontic one. The non distinction of the two levels results in falling into one of two errors: the affirmation of ontic equality denies diversity in homologation; the affirmation of ontological difference denies the equality that becomes hierarchisation.

The principle of equality is a structural principle, 'normative' and 'prescriptive', an objective to achieve: it therefore has a directive, non conclusive character. It is not a starting point or the preliminary condition that neutralises or claims to standardise diversity. On the contrary, it is the horizon of thinkability of the law, the ineliminable regulating principle, but interpretable in an articulate way according to the actual demands arising from practice. In this context, diversities must be neither ignored, nor nullified, nor even privileged: every diversity (among which even sexual diversity) is, and must be, recognised as a value. Each individual is at the same time 'different' from the others in their specificity, but 'like' the others ontologically, and therefore juridically equal.

The universal principle of equality, however, cannot be set aside from the real context of existential diversities: if different situations are treated equally indirect discriminations are introduced. Equality therefore implies the individuation of the difference, even the sexual one, and the consideration of the diversity factors, in order to offset, redress and rebalance situations of physical or social drawbacks, even by means of temporary positive actions, with norms foreseeing the support of particular existential conditions. The consideration of sexual difference asks the law on the one hand to conciliate the constitutive need for abstraction from diversity to obtain an equalisation among subjects, and on the other the concrete existential relevance of sexual identity. While it is true that man and woman must be juridically substitutable (that is, they must be granted rights recognisable to both in the same contexts and situations), it is just as undeniable that, in certain existential situations, the male and female roles are non-fungible, and therefore

---

[25] Arithmetic and quantitative justice must be integrated, as Aristotle had understood, with geometric and qualitative justice, based on the criterion of proportionality.

need differentiated rights. For the very reason that sexuality constitutively denotes being man and woman, permitting their ontological and existential identification and determining their functions, roles and ends, the law cannot but take this adequately into account. Today the law is called upon even more urgently to take charge of sexual diversity: the pressing needs of juridical feminism have intensified the problem, making at least the technical formulation of possible operational strategies urgent, if not a definitive solution.

The recognition of the need for specific protection with regard to sexual diversity is clearly relevant. Just as the law has understood the reasons for a differentiated treatment owing to the individual's different age (the minor enjoys a series of additional integrative juridical guarantees compared with the adult), sexual diversity too must be the subject of specific attention on the part of the jurist, with the formulation of a different status. The woman should have particular protection in a similar way to the minor, even though for different reasons: if the minor has been recognised a particular status insofar as a weak subject and incapable of self-protection, the woman should be guaranteed specific rights owing to her different sexual existential condition, and her different family and social role.

The law is called upon to protect the specificity of sexual diversity in the relational balance, paying attention to the distinct teleological nature of the two sexes: the female reproductive sexual sphere as a feature distinguishing the woman needs particular protection.[26] In the measure in which the specific recognition of the diversity of the sexes altered the co-existential relationship, it could not be considered authentically juridical. In this sense the claims of women's reproductive rights, ascribable to the right to the control and autonomous disposal of one's own body, are unequal as they do not take the unborn child's interests into consideration.

The jurist must hermeneutically conciliate the claims of sexual differentiation with the demands for equality, by means of a continuous dynamic comparison with the claims arising from practice, without forgetting the original meaning of the law. No technically exhaustive 'a priori' formulas exist: this does not mean that everything must be left to the will or subjective emotion. The jurist has the task of being the guardian of the correct evolution of the dynamic of the dialectic of the sexes, in the attempt to avoid the temptation of prevarication of one over the other, the unilateral prevarication of equality or difference, to confirm the relational logic, as the ineliminable condition for the affirmation of subjective identity and reciprocal recognition. At a concrete level the affirmation of the principle of equality and the right to sexual difference demand an endless effort of intermediation and the search for not only political solutions, but above all cultural and educational ones.[27]

---

[26] It must be said that at the bio-genetic level the symmetry of man and woman in the procreative process is now clear: in this sense the biological foundation is overcome, which had so tormented pre-modern thought, of the passive subjection of the woman to the active function of the male. In any case the woman's role, for the very reason that nature has endowed her with childbearing, demonstrates the need for specific protection.

[27] S.E. RHOADS, *Taking Sex Differences Seriously*, Encounter Books, New York 2002.

4.3.3 The LGBTI Claims: Equality as Equivalence

In the sphere of gender and post-gender theories reference is made to equality in an opposite way with respect to feminism. Equality is not criticised as the indifferent standardisation of difference; on the contrary, equality is appealed to in the name of the indifferent standardisation of the differences. Feminism stresses the difference between the sexes; the gender and post-gender theories deny the difference both in reference to sexual identity and to sexual orientation.

The LGBTI demands are based on the claim for the annulment of the difference between men/women/intersex/transsexual/transgender persons with respect to sexual identity which can be indifferently male, female, but also male and female or neither male nor female. But also the annulment of the difference between heterosexuals/homosexuals/bisexuals with respect to sexual orientation which can indifferently and contextually refer to individuals of the opposite sex or of the same sex.

The juridical claims of the LGBTI community are made to equality, understood as equivalence and homogenising equalisation of rights: the difference in treatment is considered discriminatory as it is based on negative irrational and unjustified prejudices of disapproval or moral censure and considered totally without any real reasonable justification. It is the claim of the anti-discriminatory right based on indistinction. Any differentiated treatment is assumed discriminating, demanding a justification of any differentiation in juridical treatment, according to the so-called 'inversion of the burden of proof'.[28]

On the contrary, tolerance is proposed as the pragmatic acceptance of every identity and sexual orientation, even minority in terms of quantity, as considered qualitatively equivalent. It is not a question of normalising diversity: the gender and post-gender theories ask to avoid any reference to what is normal and abnormal, in the name of indifferent equivalence as the only way to avoid unfair discriminations. It is the way of sexual neutrism, of the neutralisation of sex and sexuality in the name of gender, sex-less and asexual or multi-sexed and multi-sexual.

But what does discrimination mean exactly in this context? Discrimination must not be confused with distinction: discrimination means to carry out unequal treatment towards individuals or groups of individuals, putting them in an unfavourable condition or disadvantage compared with other individuals or groups. Racism, sexism, specism are all forms of discrimination in this sense: if individuals or groups of race, sex or different species are treated unequally, owing to the mere fact that they have an origin, belong to an ethnic group or species that are different, this amounts to discrimination. On its own however, the differentiated treatment towards various individuals also by reason of their ethnic, sexual or specific diversity is not discrimination.

---

[28] The juridical reasoning is not formulated in the need to demonstrate discrimination carried out by transsexuals, transgender persons or homosexuals: the discrimination is always presumed however, whenever there is a difference in treatment.

It is discrimination when the different treatment of different individuals with respect to others has no adequate or objective justification in particular circumstances. In this sense the additional protection from forms of possible exploitation of certain populations in international drug experiments is not only legitimate but dutiful, by reason of the different ethnic-social condition; maternity leave is justified by reason of the different physical-psychic-social condition of the woman with respect to the man during pregnancy; the different regulations on animal experimentation with respect to experiments carried out on human beings is justified in the balancing of risks/benefits by reason of the different specific belonging.

The LGBTI communities do not recognise their diversity (queerness), but maintain that the very fact of being considered different is discriminating, and therefore claim the same rights as cis-gender and straight persons. The annulment of every difference leads to the consideration of every different treatment unjustified: all individuals, regardless of their sexual identity and sexual orientation, must be treated—according to this standpoint—in the same way. It must not even be asked whether it is justifiable or non justifiable, since it is to be considered never justifiable and always unmotivated. The objective is the absolute neutralisation that leads to a regulation whereby any option is placed on the same level as any other, equidistantly. Equality becomes indifference of differences: it weakens the differences, making them irrelevant, in order to allow the juridical protection of diversity without producing inequalities.

In international and community documents and in some national norms an increasingly evident and visible passage can be seen. To non discrimination for reasons of age, race, social conditions and personal convictions is introduced an extensive interpretation of sex (not only as belonging to the male or female sex, but also as an individual choice) and orientation or sexual tendency is added, clearly expressing and specifying the implicit and generic indication to 'other conditions or statuses'. In other words, gender identity and sexual orientation are put on the same level as the chronological, ethnic, social, personal and ideological factor.

The choice of one's sexual identity and sexual orientation, understood as subjective choices, cannot be placed on the same level as the other elements that have been listed. Age, ethnic group, physical conditions, personal convictions are objective conditions of the person; gender identity and sexual orientation are instead subjective choices. This is a basic reason for placing them on different levels and for therefore demanding different treatment for them. It would be a discrimination to treat different situations equally, assimilating what is not assimilable, like treating equal situations differently.

The real problem is to define the boundaries of equality and non equality. No one is questioning the fact that men, women, transsexual, intersex and transgender persons are human beings in the same way as heterosexuals, homosexuals and bisexuals and, as such, have dignity that must be respected in the context of a universalistic conception of human rights. The non recognition of the dignity of those who belong to the LGBTI community in so much as human persons would be a discrimination. In this sense those who consider it necessary to refer to transgenders or to homosexuals with the expression 'transgender persons' and 'homosexual persons' are right. But what does equality and non discrimination mean and how and within what limits is such recognition normatively translated before the new claims put forward by intersexual, transgender persons, homosexuals and bisexuals?

The recognition of the dignity of the human person means the protection of their physical-psychic integrity, but also of their personal and social freedom. In other words, it means that any form of violence towards them would be intolerable, as it would also be towards heterosexual men and women. But it also means that they must have equal opportunities and must not undergo different treatment in their education, workplace, or social life. These are all acknowledgeable claims. But the acknowledgment of such claims does not automatically involve the recognition of the legal status of the intersex and transgender condition. Similarly, it does not automatically involve the equivalence of homosexual, bisexual and heterosexual unions as far as concerns marriage and the setting up of a family.

What must be stressed is the diminishing of the boundaries between the claim for 'negative freedom', or the right to express one's personal freedom without inference with access to work, public offices, social participation and politics, without limitations to free circulation to reach the partner and 'positive freedom', or the elimination of every obstacle to the full expression of personality with the recognition of a specific status or the access to marriage and filiation.[29] In this sphere equality and freedom are not competing principles, but are interacting and superimposable: equality takes on the meaning of the non discrimination of freedoms. The right to negative/positive freedom is increasingly claimed in the name of the respect for private life, personal autonomy and self-determination, in a voluntaristic horizon where individual choice is predominant with respect to the physical body which seems 'not to count' any longer before a will that tends to free itself and dis-incarnate itself from the body. A change in paradigm is taking place: while the person's first rights were based on 'habeas corpus' (since the Magna Carta in 1215), as the defence of the body from power as an indispensable step for the configuration of freedom, in the gender and post-gender theorisations the rights of freedom are claimed 'without a body', considered awkward and limiting with respect to the free expression of self.

To disagree with the 'LGBT ideology', to disapprove of it or not consider it justified, does not mean to legitimise intolerance, violence, hatred or unfair discriminations: instead it means to distinguish equally between recognisable rights and rights which demand a differentiation. To yield to every claim means to open the way to a 'slippery slope' that aims at the legitimation of every choice indifferently. To oppose the LGBTI theorisation at a theoretical level, on the basis of

---

[29] The question arises whether reasoning over the issue of the discrimination of homosexuals is not already a discrimination.

reasoning and arguments, must be allowed as the right to the freedom of conscience and the private and public expression of one's own thought.[30]

4.3.4 The Claim of the Aggravating Circumstance for Offences of Homophobia and Transphobia as a Problem

In the appeal to equality and non discrimination, the claim put forward by the LGBTI community to introduce norms foreseeing an aggravating circumstance for offences of homophobia and transphobia appears contradictory. The contradiction lies in asking for the equivalent equality of treatment with respect to heterosexual men and women on the one hand, and on the other in asking for different treatment. Their claim is juridically debatable owing to a series of reasons.

The difficulty arises from the point of view of the theory of punishment in the quantitative extension of offences and in the increase of the entity of the punishment with exclusive reference to specific 'personal motives'. Above all this widens the sphere of punishability with reference to the interior dimension (ends or motivations) without an objective empirical criterion of ascertainment, introducing the possibility of presuming the motive in subjects whose sexual behaviour is known.

Moreover, the introduction of criminal aggravating circumstances for socially disapproved acts or behaviour would constitute a moral and symbolic prevention with the purpose of promoting social awareness towards certain conditions or existential choices. The recourse to criminal law for intentions of so-called moralisation is usually criticised, whatever the contents may be, in the assumption that the law does not coincide with morals in a laical state and pluralist democracy. In such conceptual context the penal sanction foreseen by the legislator and determined/applied by the judge would take on the function of expressing the gravity of the illicit fact, with the consequence that from the entity of the punishment imposed the gravity and illicitness of the act would be deduced. The punishment would take on a moral as well as symbolic importance of representation of the value of certain assets and the disvalue of certain breaches. In such a way both the commitment relative to primary prevention would be neglected along with the search for sanctioning modalities truly capable of countering the cultural and social conditions that have had repercussions on the specific anti-juridical choices. If the objective is the education to the interiorisation of the respect of the choice of others (even sexual) in the social sphere, the way is not only the intimidatory one

---

[30] Parliamentary Assembly of the Council of Europe, *Comments on the Draft Resolution and Report on Discrimination on the Basis of Sexual Orientation and Gender Identity*, Committee on Legal Affairs and Human Rights, Rapporteur: Mr. Andreas Gross, Switzerland, Socialist Group, Doc. 12087 8 December 2009.

(with the introduction of criminal aggravation), but that of the real effective prevention of offensive acts. That could be achieved through an education in the values of sexuality and cultural development to respect behaviour that is the fruit of personal convictions, as well as the individual right to not be subjected to any form of aggression, even if this behaviour is not shared.

A further problem arises in reference to the assimilation into the law of offences committed by reason of sexual orientation and of ethnic group, race, nationality or religion and by reason of conditions of disability, age, sex. The punishment of ethnic, racial, political and religious hatred is motivated by historical reasons (we only have to think of the religious wars, Nazism and colonialism): the non acceptance of ethnocentrism or the claims of a racial, political or religious heirarchy is shared socially, following the tragic experiences of history. The punishment of hatred for the conditions of sexual belonging (women), disability or age (minors or the elderly) in a context of prevarication and subjection is not a condition that can be compared with choices of sexual orientation: they are objective and not subjective choices, characterised by the victim's intrinsic weakness and vulnerability.

The introduction of a criminal aggravation for acts against subjects in specific conditions brings with it a disparity or incongruence in treatment with respect to further possible motivations leading to equally serious acts of hatred, but perhaps even more serious. For example, if we think of acts of hatred owing to the expression of political opinions or the carrying out of a certain profession or the fact of having collaborated with justice, but also of the public manifestation of one's own sexual life of heterosexual man or woman as a value (deeming, on rational arguments, that such choice is not equivalent with respect to the transsexual or homosexual choice). There is the risk that such norm can, by generally prohibiting the discrimination of gender identity and sexual orientation, lead to intolerance towards whoever deems it dutiful to defend the relevance of nature for the law according to ethical reasons, or of the man/woman sexual difference and the heterosexual complementarity.

Furthermore, as it is not possible to ascertain the real reason leading to violence in the interiority of the mind, it would follow that whoever is the victim of violence presumably for reasons of homophobia or transphobia, would receive a privileged protection compared with whoever is subjected to violence tout court, with the negation of the principle of equality. One could then speak of 'cisphobia' or 'heterophobia', claiming adequate protection for cisgender and straight persons. Why should violence towards transsexuals, transgender persons and homosexuals be punished harder than the violence motivated by misandry (hatred towards men) or misogyny (hatred towards women)? One could also speak of 'monophobia', hatred towards dual bonds compared with 'polyphobia', hatred towards relationships of a man with more than one woman or of a woman with more than one man, but also of more than one woman with more than one man. And also of 'endophobia'/'esophobia' (hatred towards whoever has sexual relations inside or outside the family). In short the dishomogeneity of the juridical approach must be avoided, for the very reason that it is incompatible with the principle of equality (understood as parity of treatment for every human being), with respect to other possible equally hateful motivations of offensive conduct.

It must also be pointed out how the aggravating circumstances show an element of indeterminacy against the principle of legality and certainty in criminal matters. The reference to 'hatred' leaves ample room for discretionary power of interpretation: hatred is a vague word that covers offence, insult, defamation, but also violence. There is moreover the vagueness of the definition of sexuality as orientation which can refer to any preference or lifestyle. Such norm would introduce the idea that sexuality coincides with discretional if not arbitrary subjective options, legitimating the claim of sexual freedom in individual choices and relations, opening up to the liberalisation towards any sexual choice, in an equivalent and indifferent way, with indirect implications in the sphere of family law and social policy in general.[31]

4.3.5 The Law Cannot and Must Not be Indifferent

In the light of the recent social transformations and gender/queer theorisations, the law cannot but take them into account and tackle them. It is a strong provocation that forces the law to rethink itself, its role in society and its very meaning.

Such theorisations require a neutral law that is reduced to the uncritical and passive recording of merely conventional choices, dictated by the will or drives that do not bear in mind natural data at all, considering nature irrelevant or even a sham construction that can be deconstructed at pleasure. Neutral law takes on the role of the legitimation of the unlimited will to realise everything that is technologically possible and desired hedonistically, irrationally, instinctively and emotionally, considering every choice always modifiable, whatever it might be, equivalent with respect to any other possible choice. But, one asks, can the law become an extrinsic instrument of liberation of the will without limits? Individual will which rises to an ethical and juridical category, which places itself as criterion of legitimation without the recognition of any limit is the very annulment of the constitutive sense of the law.

The sense of the law cannot be identified in the subsequent indifferent recognition of individual subjective claims, whatever these may be, as if it were a mere empty recipient that can be filled with any content which collects the stratification of historical-social needs and records the transformations of practice, even the occasional ones. Neutrality is itself a stance: the standpoint of those who consider that the law must protect the will of whoever is able to express it, to claim a space for legitimacy, to assert oneself in the public debate. But the law cannot be neutral

---

[31] It must be added that for the proposed norms to be applicable they need the judicial ascertainment of the actual existence of transsexuality and homosexuality of the offended person. With the possible consequent problems of personal privacy or defence of attributions used as an excuse.

in an absolute sense, since it is structurally evaluative, because whoever uses it presupposes a value, as an alternative to the absence of law as a disvalue. If it is granted that the law is constitutively evaluative, even in a minimal sense, it means that it is called upon to protect certain values, punishing, discouraging or instead encouraging and rewarding other behaviour.

To affirm the non neutrality of the law does not mean to claim to choose one ethic by delegitimising the others from which to draw social rules, but it means to consciously assume the need to thematise the ethics 'of' or 'from' the law, the inalienable claims of lawfulness in justice, in the original sense of 'giving to every man his own'. The alternative to neutral law is not natural law in the traditional sense of the word, characterised by the claim to completely objectify self-evident truth known by man, a static, eternal and unchangeable truth, from which to systematically draw norms and values, formulating a sort of complete and non modifiable code, valid for all situations, times and places. To oppose neutral law means, instead, to critically search for the ethical structural claims within the law, to identify the modalities of justice and justification of the law dynamically, in a complex, secularised and pluralist society. It means finding and thematising the sense of the law in the dignity of each and every human being.

The law is one of the structured ways that make intersubjective relations possible and safe, guaranteeing the universal relationability of human beings as a condition of identity, the limitation of freedoms as guarantee of the compossibility of freedoms and ontological equality or equal dignity, even in existential difference, according to symmetry and reciprocity. Only the just law, which answers such requisites by objectifying the subjective claims and making them compossible, protects man: in the measure in which the law becomes the privileged absolutisation of freedom without symmetry (not recognised to others) and without reciprocity (with only rights, without duties), it goes against human beings themselves.

To oppose neutral law means to re-semanticise the principles of equality and non discrimination in the sphere of justice, revealing its non neutrality the minimum ethical assumption is referable to the dignity of every human being and to the identification of categories of individuals who deserve a specific protection by virtue of their objective conditions and not subjective choices. The task of the jurist is to laically refer to the structural juridical sense as well as to the traditional and symbolic one of the family and marriage, as guarantee of the objective structure of human identity and social coexistence. The jurist must seek a mediation between the fidelity to the anthropological needs and the dynamic adaptation to the changing of historical-social circumstances, avoiding on the one hand the crystallisation of tradition and on the other the 'slippery slope' of historicisation.

The stakes are high. This is why a careful critical rereading of the recent social transformations and gender theorisations can help us to grasp and gain awareness of the roots of certain orientations of thought that influence our very way of conceiving the law, the family and human beings. It is this awareness that will help us to make a responsible and critical choice.

Glossary

Ambisexuality undifferentiated sexual orientation towards both the opposite sex and the same sex (see bisexuality)

Androgynous individual in whom coexist, in a male or female body, appearance or behaviour belonging to both sexes

Asexed individual without sexual identity

Asexuality absence of a defined or specific sexual orientation

Biological determinism theory according to which the biological sex determines the gender in a static, fixed and non-modifiable way from birth, presupposing the coincidence and the relation of biunivocal causality between sex and gender

Biphobia hatred, refusal or irrational aversion towards bisexuality by heterosexuals and homosexuals

Bisexuality used in two senses: (a) co-presence of male and female identity, at the biological and/or psycho-social level; (b) sexual orientation towards both sexes

Cisgender individual who lives in agreement between sex (biological sexual identity) and gender (psycho-social identity)

Cross-gender crossing of genders in the identification and/or behaviour or choice to cross the male/female boundaries

Deconstructionism theory that demolishes any possibility to found a system of thought showing the contradictions of the assumptions

Disorders of sexual differentiation disorders or anomalies in the sexual development of the masculinisation or femininisation, creating states of sexual

---

The glossary has been compiled with reference to the most recurrent words in gender literature having implications in the philosophical and juridical debate. Many are new and are not even to be found in dictionaries.

indeterminacy or incongruity among the elements of the biological sex (genetic, gonadic, hormonal, phenotypic)

Environmental determinism theory according to which the gender (psycho-social identity) is constructed by the external environment

Essentialism philosophical theory which affirms the ontological priority of the universal essence over individual essence

Femininity features or psychological dispositions to act in a feminine way at a social and cultural level (also femaleness and womanhood, which denotes being female and woman)

Gender psycho-social identity which is constituted in becoming masculine/feminine

Gender bender individual that identifies himself/herself (its) with his/her (its) biological sex but considers it incomplete and transgresses the behaviour foreseen by his/her (its) gender with androgynous attitudes

Gender defender individual that defends the natural correspondence between the sex at birth and the identity and role of psycho-social gender

Gender dysphoria psycho-social distress, temporary or persistent, that an individual experiences owing to the discordance between sex (external biological sex) and gender (inwardly perceived sexual identity)

Gender identity interior and private perception of oneself as masculine/feminine

Gender normativity assumption of male or female sexual binarism as norm

Gender outlaw individual that acts according to a gender that is different from the sex, not conforming to social expectations

Gender performance action and carrying out of behaviour that expresses and represents gender identity and role

Gender performativity acting that is rooted and wears itself out in action, regardless of being, recognising the variable multiplicity of performativity

Gender role (or gender expression) external and public expression in thoughts, words, actions of one's own Gender identity, social assumption of one's own gender role

Gender socialization process of learning of gender roles in society according to social expectations

Gender variance variability and variation of the gender with reference to external behaviour, regardless of the considerations of interior distress (as opposed to 'gender dysphoria')

Genderology study of gender theories and problems

Genderqueer individuals that combine male and female elements in both body and behaviour

Hermaphrodite individual in which both male and female sexual organs and features are present together (from mythology, Hermaphrodite, the son of Hermes and Aphrodite, had the features of both sexes after being merged into a nymph)

Heteronormativity theorisation of heterosexuality as an obligatory norm to conform behaviour to, presupposing normality and superiority with respect to homosexuality

Heterophobia hatred, refusal and irrational aversion toward what is different; it can denote aversion toward those of an opposite sex or aversion towards heterosexuals

Heterosexism discrimination towards non heterosexuals by those who are heterosexual

Heterosexual privilege series of individual and institutional benefits reserved for heterosexuals

Homoparenthood being homosexual parents

Homophilia acceptance towards homosexuality

Homophobia hatred, refusal and irrational aversion towards homosexuals

Interactionism theory that thematises gender with reference both to the physical body and in relation to the interior psychic structure influenced by the external environment

Intersexual condition of sexual ambiguities (genetic, gonadic, hormonal, morphological) due to the contemporary presence of features of both sexes

LGBTI acronym of lesbians, gay, bisexuals, transgender/transsexual/transvestites, intersex persons

Masculinity psychological features of acting like a male at a social and cultural level (also maleness and manhood, which denotes being male and being man)

Monosexuality sexual attraction towards one sex only (opposite or similar)

Multiple genders (or plural genders) individual with different psycho-social gender identities

Non gendered people individuals who refuse to be defined according to a specific gender

Obligatory or compulsory heterosexuality set of institutional, cultural and social provisions which, formally and informally, reward persons in so much as they are or appear heterosexual and punish those who are not heterosexual

Pansexualism multidirectional omni-sexual attraction to individuals of the same and/or opposite sex

Polyamory living together or intimate relationship of the same sex and/or opposite sex, overcoming the dual exclusiveness of the bond

Polyandry intimate relationship of one woman with several men

Polygamy intimate relationship of one individual with several individuals of the same species of opposite sex

Polygyny intimate relationship of one man with several women

Polysexuality attraction to individuals with more than one sex

Queer (queerness queering), individual with neither male nor female identity (neither/nor), male and female (either/or; both/and) or between male and female (in between)

Sex to be physically male or female (at genetic, gonadic, hormonal, morphological level)

Sexed adjective meaning the sex in so much as incarnated in a specific male or female corporeity

Sexism discrimination of the sexes

Sexual adjective meaning 'of sex', relative to sex both as male/female distinction and as sexual preference

Sexual binarism theory that identifies sexuality in the opposite male or female duality and puts heterosexuality as hierarchically superior with respect to homosexuality

Sexual dimorphism theory that postulates the morphological difference between individuals belonging to the same species but to different sex

Sexual orientation sexual attraction or direction of sexuality regardless of sex and gender, preference with respect to the object of sexual desire

Sexual polymorphism theory that considers sexuality can be expressed in numerous, diversified and indistinct ways

Sexuality sum of desires, preferences, behaviour, gestures and attitudes aimed at the relationship with another person, in an affective and/or erotic sense (it must be distinguished from the sex act and the practice or exercise of sexuality)

Social constructionism theory maintaining that gender identity is not derived from the sex, but is a product of historical and social construction

Straight adjective referred to individuals attracted by the opposite sex, synonymous of heterosexual

Third gender condition of identity 'beyond' the male or female sexual duality

Transgender individual that expresses, transitorily or steadily, a gender identity that is not in line with the sex at birth and combines both male and female features and behaviour, wavering from one gender to the other with a partial modification of the body if needs be (trans-woman, individual that is born male and lives like a woman; trans-man individual that is born female and lives like a man)

Transphobia hatred, refusal or aversion towards transsexual and transgender persons

Transpositionism theory of the indifference of sexual orientation

Transsexual individual that lives the non correspondence between biological sex and psycho-social gender and intervenes to permanently modify their body for a complete sex reassignment (male-to-female, who passes from male to female or the femininisation of the male female-to-male; who passes from female to male or masculinisation of the female)

Transvestitism, cross-dressing phenomenon referred to individuals that have the habit of intentionally wearing publicly or privately, clothes that are usually and traditionally associated with the opposite sex

Unisexuality condition of individuals with sexual organs and features of only one sex

Unqueer (or antiqueer) individual that identifies their sex with the corresponding gender at birth

Selected Bibliography on 'Sex/gender' Debate

AA.VV (1998) The polity reader in gender studies. Polity Press, Cambridge
Ahmed S (2006) Queer phenomenology: orientations. In: Objects. Others, Duke University Press, Durham
Alsop R, Fitzsimons A, Lennon K (2005) Theorizing gender. Polity, Cambridge
Andermahr S, Lovell T, Wolkowitz C (eds) (1997) A concise glossary of feminist theory. Arnold, New York
Archer J, Lloyd B (1985) Sex and gender. Cambridge University Press, New York
Aulette JR, Wittner J, Blakely K (2008) Gendered worlds. Oxford University Press, Oxford
Beasley C (1999) What is feminism?. An introduction to feminist theory. Sage, London
Beasley C (2005) Gender and sexuality. In: Critical theories, critical thinkers. Sage, London
Beemy B, Eliason M (eds) (1996) Queer studies: a lesbian, gay, bisexual, and transgender anthology. New York University Press, New York-London
Bell AE, Sternberg RJ (eds) (1993) The psychology of gender. Guilford Press, New York
Bem SL (1981) Gender schema theory: a cognitive account of sex-typing. Psychological Rev 88: 354–364
Bem SL (1993) The lenses of gender: transforming the debate on sexual inequality. Yale University Press, New Haven
Benhabib S, Cornell D (eds) (1988) Feminism as critique: on the politics of gender. Basic Blackwell, Oxford
Benjamin J (1998) Shadow of the other. In: Intersubjectivity and gender in psychoanalysis. Routledge, New York
Benson PJ (2008) The polyamory. In: Handbook: a user's guide. AuthorHouse, Bloomington
Blasius M (ed) (2001) Sexual identities. In: Queer Politics. Princeton University Press, Princeton
Bohan HS (1997) Regarding gender: essentialism, constructionism, and feminist psychology. In: Gergen MM, Davis SN (eds) Toward a new psychology of gender. Routledge, New York
Bordo S (1990) Feminism, postmodernism and gender-scepticism. In: Nicholson L (ed) Feminism/postmodernism. Routledge, London
Bornstein K, Bear Bergman S (2010) Gender outlaws: the next generation. Avalon Publishing Group, New York
Bradly A (2007) Gender (key concept). Polity Press, Cambridge
Braidotti R (2002) Metamorphoses. In: Towards a materialistic theory of becoming. Polity Press, Cambridge
Brenkman J (2002) Queer post politics. Narrative 10(2): 174–180
Brown J (ed) (2007) The future of gender. Cambridge University Press, Cambridge
Burk C (1995) Gender. In: Power and sexuality. Routledge, London

Burr V (1995) An introduction to social constructionism. Routledge, London-New York
Butler J, Scott JW (eds) (1992) Feminists theorize the political. Routledge, New York-London
Butler J (2004c) Undoing gender. Routledge, New York
Califia P (2000) Public sex. In: The Culture of Radical Sex. Clesi Press, San Francisco
Califia P (2002) Seeking sex to power. In: The Politics of Queer Sex. Cleis Press, San Francisco
Carver T (1996) Gender is not a synonym for women. Lynne Rienne, Boulder
Carver T, Mottier V (eds) (1998) Politics of sexuality: identity. In: Gender, citizenship. Routledge, London-New York
Cealey-Harrison W, Hood-Williams J (2002) Beyond sex and gender. Sage, London
Coleman E, Gooren L, Ross N (1989) Theories of gender transpositions: a critique and suggestions for further research. J Sex Res 26: 525–538
Connell RW (1992) Gender and power. Society, the person and sexual politics, Polity, Cambridge
Corona M, Izzo D (2009) Queerdom. In: Gender displacement in a transnational context. Sestante, Bergamo
Cranny Francis A, Waring W, Stavropoulos P, Kirkby J (2003) Gender studies: terms and debate. Palgrave Macmillan, Basingstoke
Davis K, Evans M, Lorber J (2006) Handbook of gender and women's studies. Sage, London
De Beauvoir S (1949) Le deuxième sexe. Gallimard, Paris
De Lauretis T (1991) Queer theory: lesbian and gay sexualities. An introduction. Differences: J Feminist Cult Stud 3(2): iii–xviii
Degele N (2008) Gender/queer sudies. Eine Einführung. Wilhelm Fink, Stuttgart
Devor H (1989) Gender blending. In: Confronting the limits of duality. Indiana University Press, Bloomington-Indianapolis
Diamond LM (2008) Sexual fluidity. In: Understanding women's love and desire. Harvard University Press, Cambridge
Dimen M, Goldne V (eds) (2002) Gender in psychoanalytic space. Other Press, New York
Dorlin E (2008) Sexe, genre et sexualités. Presses Universitaires de France, Paris
Eadie J (ed) (2004) Sexuality. In: The essential glossary. Arnold, London
Eagly AH (1987) Sex differences in social behavior: a social role interpretation. Erlbaum, Hillsdale
Eagly AH, Wood W (1999) The origins of sex differences in human behaviour: evolved dispositions versus social roles. Am Psychologist 54: 408–423
Edwards S (1985) Gender. In: Sex and the law. Croom Helm, London
Essed P, Goldberg DT, Kobayashi A (eds) (2009) A companion to gender studies. Wiley-Blackwell, Oxford
Evans M (1990) The problem of gender for women's studies. Women's Stud Int Forum 13(5): 457–462
Feinberg L (1992) Transgender liberation: a movement whose time has come. World View Forum
Fenstermaker S, West C (eds) (2002) Doing gender, doing difference: inequality, power, and institutional change. Routledge, New York
Ferber AL, Holcomb K, Wentling T (eds) (2008) Sex, gender, and sexuality. Oxford University Press, Oxford
Ferree MM, Lorber J, Bess BB (eds) (1999) Revisioning gender. Sage, London
Finnis J (1997) Law, morality and sexual orientation. In: Corvino J (ed) Same sex: Debating the ethics, science, and culture of homosexuality. Rowman and Littlefield, London, pp 31–43
Firestone S (1970) The dialectic of sex. In: The case for feminist revolution. William Morrow and Company, New York
Flax J (1987) Postmodernism and gender relations in feminist theories. Signs 12(4): 621–643
Fox GL, Mc Bride Myrry V (2000) Gender and families. Feminist perspectives and family research. J Marriage Fam 62(4): 1160–1172
Friedan B (2001) The feminine mystique. Norton, New York
Friedman M (1991) Reclaiming the sex/gender distinction. Noûs 25(2): 200–201

Fuss D (1989) Essentially speaking: feminism. In: Nature and difference, Routledge, New York-London
Gatens M (1996) A critique of the sex/gender distinction. In: Imaginary bodies. Routledge, London
Gatens M (1989) Woman and her double(s): sex, gender and ethics. Aust Feminist Stud 10: 33–47
Gergen MM, Davis SN (eds) (1997) Toward a new psychology of gender. Routledge, New York
Giffney N, O' Rourke M (eds) (2009) The ashgate research companion to queer theory. Ashgate, Farnham
Glendon MA (2006) Family law in a time of turbolence. Martinus Nijhof, Dordrecht
Glover D, Kaplan C (2000) Genders. Routledge, New York-London
Grebowicz M (ed) (2007) Gender after Lyotard. State University of New York Press, Albany
Greer G (1970) The female eunuch. McGibbon and Keee, London
Greer G (1999) The whole woman. Alfred a Knopf, Westminister
Greer G (2003) The boy. Thames and Hudson, London
Grosz E (1994a) Experiental desire: rethinking queer subjectivity. In: Copjec J (ed) Supposing the subject. Verso, London, pp 133–157
Grosz EA (1994b) Volatile bodies: toward a corporeal feminism. University Press, Bloomington (IN)
Haynes F, KcKenna T (eds) (2001) Unseen genders: beyond the binaries. Peter Lang, New York
Halberstam J (2005) In a queer time and place. New York University Press, New York
Hall DE (2003) Queer theories. Palgrave, New York
Haritaworn J, Chin-Ju L, Klesse C (2006) Poly/logue: a critical introduction to polyamory. Sexualities 9(5): 515–529
Harper C (2007) Intersex. Berg, Oxford-New York
Hartmann H (2005) Gendering politics and policy. Haworth Political Press, New York
Harrison WC, Hood-Williams J (2002) Beyond sex and gender. Sage, London
Hausman B (1995) Changing sex: transexualism, technology, and the idea of gender. Duke University Press, Durham
Hausman B (2001) Recent transgender theory. Feminist Stud 27(2): 465–490
Hawkesworth M (1997) Confounding gender. Sign 22(3): 649–685
Herdt G (1994) Third sex, third gender: beyond sexual dimorphism in culture and history. Basic Books, New York
Hird MJ (2009) Biologically queer. In: Giffney N, O' Rourke M (eds) The Ashgate research companion to queer theory. Ashgate, Farnham, pp 347–362
Hird MJ (2000) Gender's nature: intersexuality, transexualism and the 'sex'/'gender' binary. Feminist Theory 2(3): 347–364
Holmes M (2010) Critical intersex. Ashgate, Farnham
Hopkins PD (ed) (1998) Sex/machine. In: Readings in culture, gender, and technology. Indiana University Press, Bloomington (Indiana)
Hurtig MC, Kail M, Rouch H (eds) (1991) Sexe et genre. De la hiérarchie entre les sexes. CNRS, Paris
Jackson S, Scott S (2010) Theorizing sexuality. Open University Press, New York
Jackson S (1998) Theorizing gender and sexuality. In: Jackson S, Jones J (eds) Contemporary feminist theories. New York University Press, New York, pp 134–137
Johnson P (1998) Sexism. In: Encyclopaedia of applied ethics. Academic, San Diego-London, vol IV, pp 65–73
Kaplan C, Glover D (1998) Genders. Routledge, London
Keating AL (2002) Gender. In: Summers J (ed) Glbtq: an encyclopaedia of gay, lesbian, transgender, and queer culture. New England Publishing Associates, Chicago
Kessler SJ, McKenna W (1978) Gender: an ethnomethodological approach. Wiley, New York
Kimmel M (2004) The gendered society. Oxford University Press, New York

Kipnis K, Diamond M (1998) Paediatric ethics and the surgical assignment of sex. J Clin Ethics 9(4): 398–410
Kirsch MH (2000) Queer theory and social change. Routledge, London
Kitzinger C (1999) Intersexuality: deconstructing the sex/gender binary. Feminism Psychology 9(4): 493–498
Kroll R (hrsg) (2002) Lexikon. Gender studies, Geschlechterforschung. Ansätze, Personen, Grundbegriffe, Verlag J.B. Metzler, Stuttgart Weimer
Kuby G (2007) Die gender revolution. Relativismus in Aktion, Fe-medienverlag GmbH, Kisslegg
Lancaster RN, Di Leonardo M (eds) (1997) The gender/sexuality reader. In: Culture, history, political economy. Routledge, New York-London
Layton L (1998) Who's that girl? Who's that boy?. Clinical practice meets postmodern gender theory. Jason Aronson, Northvale
Lehne GK (2003) Gender identity. In: Ponzetti JJ (ed) International encyclopaedia of marriage and family. MacMillan, New York , vol II, pp 728–232
Lévy-Strauss C (1947) Les structures elementaires de la parenté. Presses Universitaires de France, Paris
Lips HM (2001) Sex and gender: an introduction. Mayfield, Mountain View
Lloyd G (1989) Woman as other: sex, gender and subjectivity. Aust Feminist Stud 10:13–22
Lorber J (1994) Paradoxes of gender. Yale University Press, New Haven
MacKinnon C (2006) Difference and dominance. In: Hackett E, Haslanger S (eds) Theorizing feminism. Oxford University Press, Oxford
Martin B (1994) Sexualities without genders and other queer Utopias. Diacritics 24(2/3): 104–121
Maynard M, Purvis J (eds) (1995) Hetero(sexual) politics. Taylor and Francis, Bristol
Meijer I, Prins B (1998) How bodies come to matter?: an interview with Judith Butler. Signs 23(2): 275–289
Meyers DT (ed) (1997) Feminist social thought: reader. Routledge, New York-London
Millett K (1969) Sexual politics. University of Illinois Press, Urbana-Chicago
Mitchell J (1973) Woman's estate. Vintage Books, New York
Mitchell J (1966) Women: the longest revolution. New Left Review, Boston
Mogge-Grotjahn H (2004) Gender, sex und gender studies. Freiburg i.B, Eine Einführung, Lambertus
Money J (1970) Matched pairs of hermaphrodites: behavioural biology of sexual differentiation from chromosomes to gender identity. Eng Sci 33: 34–39
Moreau S (2010) What is discrimination?. Philos Public Aff 143–179
Morland I, Willox A (eds) (2005) Queer theory. Palgrave MacMillan, New York
Nestle J, Howell C, Wilchins R (eds) (2002) GenderQueer: voices from beyond the sexual binary. Alyson Books, Los Angeles
Nicholson L (ed) (1990) Feminism/postmodernism. Routledge, London
Nicholson L (2000) Gender. In: Jaggar AM, Young IM (eds) A companion to feminist philosophy. Blackwell, Oxford, pp 289–297
Nicholson L (1994) Interpreting gender. Sign 20(1): 79–105
Nussbaum MC (2010) From disgust to humanity. In: Sexual Orientation & Constitutional Law. Oxford University Press, Oxford
Nussbaum MC (2006) Hiding from humanity: disgust, shame, and the law (2004). Princeton University Press, Princeton
Nussbaum MC The professor of parody. The new republic online, 22/02/99
O' Leary D (1997) The gender agenda. In: Redefining equality. Vital Issue Press, Lafayette (Louisiana)
O'Flaherty M, Fisher J (2008) Sexual orientation, gender identity and international human rights law: contextualising the Yogyakarta principles. Human Rights Law Rev 8(2): 207–248
Oakley A (1972) Sex, gender and society. Martin Robertson, Oxford
Okin SM (1989) Justice. In: Gender and the family. Basic books, New York

Ortner SB, Whitehead H (1981) Sexual meanings: the cultural construction of gender and sexuality. Cambridge University Press, Cambridge
Phoca S (2000) Feminism and gender. In: Gamble S (ed) The Routledge critical dictionary of feminism and postfeminism. Routledge, New York
Pilcher J, Whelehan I (2004) 50 key concepts in gender studies. Sage, London
Pocha S (2001) Feminism and gender. In: Gamble S (ed) The Routledge companion to feminism and postfeminism. Routledge, London
Preves SE (2003) Intersex and identity: the contested self. Rutgers University Press, New Brunswick
Reiner W (1997) To be male or female: that is the question. Arch Paediatr Adolesc Med 151: 224–225
Rhode DL (1989) Justice and gender. In: Sex discrimination and the law. Harvard University Press, Cambridge
Rhode DL (1990) Theoretical perspectives on sexual difference. New Haven, London
Rice Wood k, Scales Rostosky s, Remer p (2003) Gender. In: Ponzetti JJ (ed) International encyclopaedia of marriage and family. MacMillan, New York, vol II, pp 723–728
Rich A (1980) Compulsory heterosexuality and lesbian existence. Signs 5: 631–660
Richardson D (ed) (1996) Theorizing heterosexuality. Open University Press, Buckingham
Richardson D (2001) Sexuality and gender. In Smelser NJ, Baltes PB (eds) International encyclopaedia of the social and behavioural sciences. Elsevier, New York-Oxford, pp 14.018–14.021
Rothblatt M (1995) The Apartheid of Sex. In: A Manifesto on the Freedom of Gender. Crown Publishers, New York
Rubin G (1994) Sexual traffic (interview with Judith Butler). Differences: J Feminist Cult Stud 6(2/3): 62–99
Rubin G (2006) The traffic in women: notes on the "political economy" of sex. In: Lewin E (ed) Feminist anthropology. A Reader, Blackwell, Oxford
Rubin G (1984) Thinking sex: Notes for a radical theory of the politics of sexuality. In: Vance CS (ed) Pleasure and danger: exploring female sexuality. Routledge and Kegan Paul, New York
Scott J (1999) Some reflections on gender and politics. In: Ferrée M, Lorber J, Hess B et al (eds) Revisioning gender. Sage-Thousand Oaks, CA
Scott JW (1986) Gender: a useful category of historical analysis. Am Historical Rev 91(5): 1053–1075
Seideman S (1997) Difference troubles: queering social theory and sexual politics. Cambridge University Press, Cambridge
Seideman S (1996) Queer theory/sociology. Blackwell, Oxford
Seideman S (2003) The social construction of sexuality. Norton and Company, New York
Seidman S (1997) Difference trouble: queering social theory and sexual politics. Cambridge University Press, Cambridge
Shaver P, Hendrick C (1987) Sex and gender. Sage, London
Shaw A, Ardener S (2005) Changing sex and bending gender. Berghahn Books, New York
Showalter E (1989) Speaking of gender. Routledge, London
Sommers CH (1997) Who stole feminism?. Simon and Schuster, New York
Sowle Cahill L (1996) Sex, gender and christian ethics. Cambridge University Press, Cambridge
Stone A (2007) An introduction to feminist philosophy. Polity, Malden, Cambridge
Stychin C (2003) Governing sexuality: the changing politics of citizenship and law reform. Hart Publishing, London
Stryker S, Whittle S (2006) The transgender study reader. Routledge, New York
Sytsma SS (ed) (2006) Ethics and intersex. Springer, Dordrecht
Tarrant S (2006) When sex became gender. Routledge, London
Thompson D (1989) The sex/gender distinction: a reconsideration. Aust Feminist Stud 10: 23–31
Tong R (1998) Feminist thought: a more comprehensive introduction. Allen and Uniwin, Sidney
Turner WB (2000) A genealogy of queer theory. Temple University Press, Philadelphia

Valocchi S (2005) Not yet queer enough: the lessons of queer theory for the sociology of gender and sexuality Gender and Society, vol 19, 6, pp 750–770

Varikas E (2006) Penser le sexe et le genre. Presses Universitaires de France, Paris

Walgenbach K, Dietze D, Hornscheidt A, Palm K (2007) Gender als interdependente Kategorie. Neue Perspektive auf Intersektionalität, Diversität und Heterogeneität, Verlag Barbara Budrich, Opladen and Farmington Hills

Warner M (1999) The trouble with normal. In: Sex, politics, and the ethics of queer life, Simon and Schuster, New York

Warner M (ed) (1993) Fear of a queer planet: queer politics and social theory. University of Minnesota Press, Minneapolis

Warnke G (2007) After identity. In: Rethinking race, sex, and gender. Cambridge University Press, Cambridge

Warnke G (2010) Debating sex and gender (Fundamental of Philosophy). Oxford University Press, Oxford

Wearing B (1996) Gender: the pleasure and pain of difference, Longman, Victoria

Weber L (2009) Understanding race, class, gender, and sexuality: a conceptual framework. Oxford University Press, Oxford

Weeks J (1995) Invented moralities. In: Sexual values in an age of uncertainty. Polity Press, Cambridge

West C, Zimmerman DH (1987) Doing gender, gender and society, 1, pp 125–151

Wilchins R (2004) Queer theory, gender theory: an instant primer. Alyson, Los Angeles

Witt C (2011) The metaphysics of gender. Oxford University Press, Oxford

Wollstonecraft M (1792) A vindication of the rights of women

Young IM (1990) Justice and the politics of difference. Princeton University Press, Princeton

Young IM (2009) Lived body versus gender. In: Essed P, Goldberg DT, Kobayashi A (eds) A companion to gender studies. Wiley-Blackwell, Oxford, pp 102–113

Printed in Great Britain
by Amazon